Talking It Out

A Guide to Groups for Abused Women

by Ginny NiCarthy, Karen Merriam
and Sandra Coffman

The Seal Press

New Leaf Series

Seal Press
P.O. Box 13
Seattle, WA 98111

Library of Congress Cataloging in Publication Data

NiCarthy, Ginny.
  Talking it out.

  Copyright by Ginny NiCarthy, Karen Merriam, and Sandra Coffman.
  Bibliography: p. 153
  1. Family violence. 2. Abused wives—Services for. 3. Self-help
groups. 4. Group counseling. 5. Group relations training. I. Merriam, Karen. II. Coffman, Sandra. III. Title.
HQ809.N53 1984   362.8′2   84-23494
ISBN 0-931188-24-5

Book and cover design by Rachel da Silva
Typeset in Modern by The Franklin Press

First Edition, November 1984
10 9 8 7 6 5

Acknowledgements

This book would not have been possible without the enduring courage and honesty of the women who attended the mutual support groups we led. Their experiences, wisdom, strength and knowledge inform every part of our work. We regret that we can't give public credit to the many group participants who have helped us in our work because of the danger such disclosure could cause them.

New Beginnings Shelter for Battered Women has sponsored the group meetings described in this book for over three years. We are grateful to Nanette Westerman for her consistent encouragement to provide this valuable outreach and community service. We also wish to give special thanks to the childcare staff trained by the Shelter to work with our community group, including Nije, Ann and Jill. They have been so effective in their work that some of the children have told us they wanted to come to their group even when their moms were reluctant to attend theirs.

The generous donation by the YWCA of the rooms for the weekly group meetings and childcare contributed greatly to the viability of the group. We wish to thank Tina Narr, Mary Hess and the counseling staff who offered invaluable cooperation and support in providing a safe and consistent meeting place.

Addei Fuller, Marianne Pettersen and Bernadette Willman contributed significantly to the continuing growth of the group model. They created new formats, developed new exercises and enriched our understanding of the needs of special populations.

Many women contributed a great deal of time and thought to reviewing our manuscript. Their comments were stimulating and challenging, and were always valuable. Whenever

possible we incorporated the needed changes or new ideas su
gested by our critics. We thank the following women for sharir
with us their time, knowledge and critical attention: Sharo
Atkins, Karen Bosley, Julia Boyd, Donna Cooper, Marie Fortun(
Addei Fuller, Linda Gidding, Naomi Gottlieb, Ann Harvey
Marcia Macomber, Ruth McCormick, Wadiyah Nelson, Juli
Pascoe, Marianne Pettersen, Marilyn Smith and Bernadett
Willman.

In addition, Karen Merriam would like to thank the follow
ing women whose support and encouragement nurtured and
sustained her work: Carol Maicki, Rosemary Echols, Lori Mc-
Kenna, Valerie Kaminski, Nancy Athene, Mary Baker, Judy
Vanderyn, Hester Witchey and Robin Armstrong.

Faith Conlon, Rachel da Silva, and Barbara Wilson of Seal
Press gave us encouragement, criticism and congratulations at
each critical step in the process of developing this manuscript.
As our principal editor, Faith Conlon exhibited supreme patience and diplomatic skill in forging compromises between the
three authors. Her insistence on quality of presentation has
been as unyielding as it has been gentle. We are sincerely
grateful for her assistance.

Finally, we would like to thank Rosalie Sable, who has typed
many drafts of the manuscript, meeting hurried deadlines and
wrestling with a sometimes uncooperative computer. Rosalie
often turned chaos into order, and she gave us some invaluable
editorial suggestions.

Contents

Dedicated,
with respect and admiration,
to the thousands of women who are
"talking it out" in support groups,
ιelping each other to forge new lives of peace and justice.

Introduction

This book was planned as a short article that would describe just a few exercises we have created and used successfully with groups for battered women. We wanted to respond to the many requests we received from local students, shelter staff, mental health professionals and a wide range of our referral sources for information about our group work. The exercises, we thought, were the only "new" ideas we had to offer.

As we began our writing, however, we looked about in journals, books and "trade papers" for theoretical models and practical techniques to which we could refer our readers to supplement our limited offering. We found that although there is separate information about group work, about abuse and about the politics of battering, there is no *single resource* that addresses the questions we believe are important for group leaders. The major questions we have tried to answer in this book are:

1. What are the social, political and personal issues unique to group work with abused women?
2. What techniques are the most helpful in conducting groups for abused women? How do they relate to political and social issues, as well as to group work theory?
3. How does a leader or organizer get a group started? What exactly does the leader do in a group meeting?
4. What special concerns and needs arise in groups for women of color, for women of faith, for lesbians, or for women of different abilities, ages and backgrounds?
5. How can leaders avoid burnout and actually enjoy leading groups for abused women?

Thus, with a mixture of excitement and dread, we abandoned the safer limitations of an article and committed ourselves to the adventure of communicating our answers to these questions as fully as possible. Seal Press gave us strong encouragement and supported us at each step with their own commitment to publish a series of books (The New Leaf Series) devoted to helping abused women.

In this book we describe our group model for working with battered women. The model we present, which is based on both our experience and our theoretical orientation, is a feminist, all-women, women-led, mutual-help, drop-in group. We think that a group format is often the best way of providing support and information, while also decreasing the intense isolation of women who've been abused. Regardless of the mode, however —group, individual, couples or family counseling—the *safety* of the abused woman is, for us, the primary concern. If violent or abusive behavior has been disclosed, the counseling must be designed to protect the safety of the victim and assert the responsibility and accountability of the abuser for the violent behavior.

In the shared work of writing this book, as in our co-leadership of our group for abused women, we have many times disagreed with each other. Often we have compromised. Always we have learned from each other. We come from different disciplines —social work and psychology—and our differing approaches to therapy and counseling may be described as cognitive-behavioral, humanistic, psychodynamic and feminist. What unites us is our active desire and willingness to learn from other women about the causes and forms of violence against women, and to contribute toward the larger effort to end battering and other kinds of abuse of women. As co-authors we express another kind of commitment that we hope the reader will share: to explore, develop and describe both the evolving responses to the abuse of women that we found effective and the ideas that inform those responses. We have found that our co-leadership and our co-authorship have required great flexibility. We encourage you, too, to remain flexible as you explore our contributions. Take from our work only what may be useful for you. We are presenting only one model. Others have developed different models, which work well in their communities.

While we have confidence that what we have learned and implemented can be of value to others and can be applied to other group situations, our conclusions and suggestions come from our experience, not from a controlled study. Although we have witnessed many positive responses to our work, we have not formally tested or evaluated it. We hope others will now subject our model to more rigorous testing.

We have kept references in the text to a minimum. Our primary goal throughout has been to make the information as accessible as possible without compromising accuracy or thoroughness. We hope that this book will assist those who teach, train or supervise. It can guide agency administrators, grassroots organizers, shelter workers, mental health workers, feminist therapists, women who have been abused, and students. We think that workers who lead incest groups or other kinds of groups for survivors of sexual violence will also find this book helpful.

Our Experience

If you use this book for training or as a guide for your own work, keep in mind that the drop-in group that we co-led was composed, as far as we know, almost exclusively of heterosexual women. Women of color were generally underrepresented when compared with the proportion in the general population of the city. Also, this was (and remains) an urban group, although some women came from suburbs twenty miles away to attend the meetings. The average number of women attending each meeting was nine, although we had a few weeks in which sixteen or eighteen women "dropped in." Rarely were there meetings with fewer than five women attending. We found that we had no ability to predict who might attend from week to week, and there was no discernible preponderance of members from one economic, social or educational group.

The group that we co-led was founded in 1976 by one of us, was led or co-led by all of us for some period of time, and currently continues to be led by another of us. The group has been a community "arm" of a local shelter for abused women, and funding to pay for group leaders and child care has been channelled through the shelter. We mention these factors, and the additional information that we are white, middle-class, professional women who have had some experiences with physical and emotional abuse in our personal lives, but have not been battered, to provide a context for you to consider as you read. Throughout the book we remind you to adapt our suggestions or style to fit your own leadership style, community needs or group composition. We do not suggest, however, that you adapt or change the basic feminist principles and understandings on which our work is firmly based.

Content of the Book

In Part One, we explore and describe in some depth the
fundamental concepts that guide our work, with an emphasis
on the evolution of the social response to battering in conjunc-
tion with the feminist movement. Part One also attempts to
answer the second question posed at the beginning of this
Introduction, discussing the self-help movement and the development of our "mutual-help," drop-in group model.

Part Two offers concrete information about strategies for
starting a group to assist community leaders, agency personnel,
community activists and women who are preparing to lead a
group. Part Three is a nuts-and-bolts guide for the group leader.
In this section, we suggest a way to structure the group meeting;
we also describe some of the individual and group composition
problems that may arise during a meeting and offer suggestions
on how to handle them. Next we present some topics that are
often useful to discuss in the group, as well as some brief exercises. We end the section by detailing five group exercises that
we have used successfully with our groups. We take you step by
step through the process of presenting each exercise in the
group meeting.

Part Four describes some considerations essential for
groups of women who may desire or require approaches different from those we suggest earlier. Although the exercises in this
book are designed primarily for women in heterosexual relationships, we feel the material is relevant to lesbians involved
with abusive partners and that it is adaptable to groups for
lesbians. We specifically offer ideas for groups for women of
color, lesbians, women of faith, women of differing abilities,
teen-agers and recovering alcoholics. We also describe "second
phase" groups and the "group of two." Finally, we discuss the
subject of leadership "burnout." We describe a social and political perspective as well as the individual experience of this
phenomenon.

Our "Final Thoughts," with which we conclude the book,
are those with which we now also begin the book. We are pleased
to share our creative process and work with you, and we hope
you will be inspired to enjoy your own creativity as you teach
and work to end violence against women.

Talking It Out

Part One

Groups for Abused Women:
A Feminist Movement

Chapter 1

Abused Women: Past and Present

Since the mid-1970s, groups for women who are abused or battered have been an important resource both in and out of shelters. Whether the group emphasizes problem-solving, support, therapy, education or consciousness-raising, it offers advantages not available from individual therapy or other services.

We are advocating a feminist, all-women, women-led, mutual-help, drop-in model, which draws on several historical roots for its methods, goals and purposes. In this and the following two chapters, we will explain the origins and underlying principles of some of our viewpoints by placing the model in a context of the separate histories of violence against women, the development of the battered women's and shelter movement, feminism and feminist therapy, and the self-help movement.

Traditional Views of Battered Women

Until the last decade, mental health, religious, medical and law and justice professionals accepted and perpetuated misleading stereotypes about women who remain with men who batter them. Many of those judgments were based on historical notions, more or less consistent for many centuries, about the place of women in society, their capabilities (or presumed lack of them) and appropriate treatment of them by authority figures—especially husbands.

As the disciplines of sociology and psychology developed, researchers and practitioners in the fields of family relations and of violent behavior continued to operate on those established judgments. They generally assumed that violence in the family was either a rare aberration or was brought about by the behavior or attitudes of the victim. Between 1939 and 1969, there was not a single reference to violence indexed in the *Journal of Marriage and the Family*.[1] In 1944 the influential psychiatrist Helene Deutsch wrote about women's "masochistic" needs, alleging that battered women loved brutal men *because* of their brutality.[2]

These attitudes of professionals reflected the views held by most people before the recent wave of the feminist movement. Friends and relatives of women who were battered refused to recognize what was occurring. "Whoever those battered women are, if they really do exist, they're certainly not like anyone *I* know," was the sentiment that best defended against any threat of the problem coming too close to home. Nearly all battered women were ashamed to admit what had been done to them, and if they did talk about the abuse, they risked further blame from friends or relatives. Their silence reinforced most people's beliefs that battering didn't happen, or happened to people who didn't count. And when women who were battered heard those beliefs expressed, their shame increased still further and their commitment to silence about the abuse intensified.

Feminists publicly recognized the problem of wives' servitude to their "masters" as early as the 1848 Women's Rights Convention at Seneca Falls and were incensed at husbands' rights to "chastise" their wives.[3] Nineteenth-century and early twentieth-century feminists made periodic efforts to call attention to wife battering and to prevent it, but not until the "second wave" of the feminist movement was there a sustained effort to focus on the problem.

The Battered Women's and Shelter Movement

The many social changes of the 1960s and 1970s brought a shift in the central issues of the women's movement, including work against sexual and other interpersonal violence against women. As the feminist movement grew during the 1960s, women came together in consciousness-raising groups, where they gained awareness that many of their problems were not simply personal, but political. Women who had learned to view each other primarily as competitors for the attention of men began to speak honestly to each other about their private lives. They found strength and solace in their shared experiences and newly acquired common understanding.

By the early 1970s fresh perspectives on male-female relationships resulted in an analysis of rape as an act of power, rather than of sex. Speak-outs on rape enabled many women to admit, for the first time, that they had been sexually victimized, in some cases by boyfriends or acquaintances. The myth of the rapist as stranger began to dissolve. The anti-rape movement flourished, rape crisis centers proliferated, and for the first time, many women understood that women victimized by rapists were not the appropriate people to blame for the crime. They realized that forced sex is rape, even if the perpetrator is a boyfriend, and even if the woman has previously had sex with the man.It would take another ten years or more for women to name husbands' coercive sex "rape."

Most women, however, still owed their primary loyalty to their men. Many women who were battered by their husbands had yet to admit that it was happening and were far from realizing that their best hope for survival was to leave the violent men. Moreover, even the rapid social changes of the 1960s and early 1970s had not removed the major stumbling block for women who considered moving out on their own: There were still no safe places for them to go.

In England and the United States some services for homeless or destitute women had been provided by religious and other organizations before the 1970s. But social service agencies neither recognized battering as a major social problem nor made a concerted effort to reach out to the victims.

In 1971 a grassroots group of women in a district on the outskirts of London organized the first shelter for women who were escaping from violent men. (Erin Pizzey was the charismatic leader of this group and became an important organizer in the movement. Later she turned against the feminist movement and revised her original ideas in ways that many feminists believe perpetuate the old notions that women who are battered "ask for it.")

It took three or four years for the shelter movement to cross the Atlantic, but by the mid-1970s shelters and Safe Homes for women who had been battered were springing up throughout the United States. The word had spread that shelters in England were overflowing with women and children as soon as their doors were opened. In the United States, individual women began to speak up about the abuse they had endured, and researchers for the first time began to question women about their experiences. Their answers were hard to believe at first, but soon it was impossible to deny the evidence that between one-third and one-half of women would at some time be subjected to violence by their intimate partners.[4] Further questions made it clear that about 25 percent of men and women accepted some degree of violence between spouses as necessary, good or normal.[5]

Feminists and other grassroots groups refused to accept violence against women or children as inevitable or desirable, and began to organize against it. In 1975 the National Organization for Women formed a task force on battered women. By 1977 the National Women's Conference in Houston provided women who had begun to open shelters and Safe Homes all over the U.S. the opportunity to compare their experiences, problems and plans. It was at this conference that the groundwork was laid for the national movement to end domestic violence. The previous year had witnessed the publication of Betsy Warrior's *Working On Wife Abuse*, a directory of services for battered women, and Del Martin's important book, *Battered Wives*. The movement was afoot in a big way.[6]

As battered women began to see the need to leave their abusive partners, it became clear to feminists, professional therapists, grassroots activists and some traditional social service administrators that the women needed a place to go if they chose to leave home. "Safe Homes" were often the first step. A Safe Home is a private residence in which a woman can stay for a few days among people, usually a family, who understand and empathize with her situation. The cost for establishing Safe Homes is relatively low, which was particularly important for the early domestic violence programs, as they were often staffed by volunteers who used personal telephones as crisis lines.

Shelters

In some areas, especially rural districts, Safe Homes remained the housing of choice, but where money was available to house several families in one building and hire staff, Safe Home organizations often became shelter systems. A shelter was frequently a run-down rental apartment, housing two or three mothers and their children. As financing improved, sometimes houses were bought and, in a few cases, even built for specific use as shelters. In some areas, large residences, such as YWCAs or religious hostels, were turned into shelters.

Shelters offer more than a safe place to stay. They provide

time to think and time away from confusing demands and emotional turmoil, information about practical help from public and private agencies, and support from staff and other residents. It's hard to characterize shelters because each is different from the next and because the particular individuals who are housed during any week create a unique atmosphere.

For some women the strange surroundings, the mix of ethnicity, lifestyles and other women's children poses greater difficulties in coping than does the familiar threat of violence, and they soon leave. Others find that something special happens when a group of women in like circumstances are suddenly cast into a common living situation, trading advice, childcare and stories of their lives. The women and children gain understanding of their common circumstances and bolster each other's courage. Women who feared they were "crazy" are daily confronted with the presence of others who share similar dreams, fears, regrets and feelings of shame, and yet who seem quite sane. "Perhaps," they begin to think, "I'm not crazy, after all."

For some women change begins when they worry about other shelter residents who don't fully recognize the danger they're in. They begin to see the similarities between other women and themselves and gradually, by observing and interacting with each other, advance to wondering if their own lives are more at risk than they had wanted to believe. Once the reality of their own danger is realistically assessed, they are often compelled to seek a more permanent way out of it and are helped by other residents and staff who provide models of living in safety.

Living in a shelter causes some women to re-evaluate their status as women. Living together for a week or a month, women experience, often for the first time, the strange sensation of freedom from male domination. They see with greater clarity the meaning of economic discrimination and deprivation and the limitations of sex-role socialization, especially the roles of mother and wife.

Shelters were organized by women with many different political perspectives and backgrounds. Although traditional agencies like the Salvation Army established some of the early shelters, and some were begun by non-feminists who were simply concerned about women in intolerable relationships, most of the early shelters were begun by feminists or women who were able to work within a feminist framework.

Susan Schechter notes in *Women and Male Violence* that formerly battered women, who were major organizers of some shelters, were not likely to be feminists. She points out: "But, whatever specific label, if any, battered women use, they brought what one woman called 'gut-felt' commitments into the movement. . . . Their experience, strengths, and scars were the force that started the movement."[7]

As women working on crisis hotlines or in women's centers listened to more and more women who were battered, they realized the desperate need for a place to safely house the women. But, the more they heard, the more frustrated they became about the pervasive indifference of the institutions that might have helped. Schechter recalls her own experience:

> All I can remember is phone calls, constant, never-ending calls from battered women with no place to go and with endless stories of institutional indifference. . . . Working with battered women and not being able to help them to find what they concretely need creates a panic, a steady stream of adrenaline that continues until help is found. . . . We had to assess safety, give her support and information, and help her weigh alternatives. Maybe for shelter workers who can offer a safe place, the feelings are different, but all we had was a crisis phone.[8]

The Broadening Movement

It became obvious that shelters were essential, but it didn't take long for shelter workers to realize that they could not answer all of the women's concerns, including some that Schechter alludes to in the paragraph above. As shelter and hotline workers from different communities met at conferences and compared experiences, they became convinced that housing was a solution to just one part of the problem, and more systematic responses to battering would have to be made on state levels. Welfare policies and laws on spouse assault, child support and ownership of property by married couples would all have to be changed in order for women to have the economic options enabling them to leave violent men. Women who had counted on having economic support from men for the rest of their lives would need education or training to support themselves and their children.

On a more immediate level they needed legal advice from professionals who understood their special situations and who wouldn't demand money right away. They needed to know that if they called police, the officers would come; if they had a restraining order, it would mean something to the police; if they reported assault, the man would be prosecuted; and if they were willing to go through the legal process, they would be supported in their efforts. They wanted to know there was some hope that men could be helped to change if they wanted to.

Also needed was a method of distributing information and comparing ideas among the people doing the work to keep each organization from needing to reinvent the wheel, and to promote changes on a national level.

A national newsletter, begun in 1976, was later combined with an anti-rape newsletter and evolved into *Aegis: The Magazine on Ending Violence Against Women.*[9] This remains a principal organ for the movement against violence against women, providing information and notices about resources. It also offers a forum for discussing much of the movement's political vision, or more properly, visions. *Response to Violence in the Family and Sexual Assault*[10] is another important journal, describing innovative and successful programs and providing information on national funding and legislation.

In 1978 the National Coalition Against Domestic Violence (NCADV) was formed in Washington, D.C., and the first national membership conference was held in 1980.   A second NCADV conference in 1982 brought both unity and a deepened awareness that there is great diversity among the groups and individuals in the movement—a diversity that must continually be recognized, respected and confronted. The Coalition has a commitment to meet the needs and enhance participation of women of color and lesbians, as well as formerly battered women. Leaders and group members who work within the framework of this national—and growing *international*—movement gain courage from it to continue to help each other create safe lives.

Notes

1. John O'Brien, "Violence in Divorce Prone Families," *Journal of Marriage and the Family*, 33 (Nov. 1971), pp. 692–698 cited in Richard J. Gelles, *The Violent Home* (Beverly Hills: Sage Publications, 1974), p. 20.

2. Helene Deutsch, *Psychology of Women*, Vol. I (New York: Grune and Stratton, 1944), p. 276.

3. Robin Morgan, ed., *Sisterhood is Powerful:An Anthology of Writings from the Women's Liberation Movement* (New York: Random House, 1970), p. 15.

4. Estimates vary widely. Murray A. Straus, Richard J. Gelles and Suzanne K. Steinmetz, extrapolating from an extensive survey, suggest that "about a third of all American couples experience a violent incident every year, and about two thirds have experienced such an incident at least once in the marriage." See *Behind Closed Doors: Violence in the American Family* (New York: Anchor Press/Doubleday, 1980), p. 48.

Jennifer Baker Fleming says "researchers predict that one or more violent episodes will occur in the course of 50 per cent of American marriages ..." See *Stopping Wife Abuse* (New York: Anchor Press/ Doubleday, 1979), p. 10.

Lenore Walker estimates that "as many as 50 [percent]" of all women will be battering victims at some point in their lives. See *The Battered Woman* (New York: Harper & Row, 1979), p. v.

5. Straus, Gelles and Steinmetz, op. cit., p. 47.

6. Betsy Warrior, *Working on Wife Abuse* (Cambridge, MA: Seventh Supplemented Edition, 1978) and Del Martin, *Battered Wives* (San Francisco: Glide Publications, 1976). For a thorough analysis of the shelter movement, see Susan Schechter's book *Women and Male Violence* (Boston: South End Press, 1982).

7. Schechter, op. cit., pp. 49–50.

8. Ibid, p. 70.

9. *Aegis: The Magazine on Ending Violence Against Women.* (Washington, D.C.: National Communications Network, the Feminist Alliance Against Rape, and the Alliance Against Sexual Coercion, P.O. Box 21033, Washington, D.C. 20009).

10. *Response to Violence in the Family and Sexual Assault.* (Washington, D.C.: Center for Women Policy Studies, 2000 P Street, Suite 508, Washington, D.C. 20036.)

Chapter 2

Changing Theories
of Battering

As the grassroots feminist shelter movement was growing, some academic theorists were breaking new ground in studying violence in the family. Early in the 1970s Murray Straus and Richard Gelles published the controversial finding that violence against children and spouses by family members was far more common than had been previously recognized. They concluded that the home was more often a battleground than the peaceful haven popularly assumed and that the marriage license appeared to be a hitting license. Their work was particularly useful in publicizing the pervasiveness of battering (and child abuse) and in emphasizing that such violence is supported by social institutions.[1]

Straus, Gelles and their colleague Susan Steinmetz have been criticized by feminists for the limitations of their quantitative approach to domestic violence, particularly their tendency to normalize violence between spouses and to obscure the significance of the imbalance of power between husbands and wives. By concentrating on the tabulation of acts of violence, they have underestimated the significance of degrees of violence and the ways that the kinds of violence affect power in relationships. Although Straus has noted the role of sexism in violence, neither he nor Gelles nor Steinmetz has integrated the historical context of patriarchal institutions into their work.

Feminist Theories of Battering

Feminist sociologists R. Emerson Dobash and Russell P. Dobash have forcefully presented the necessity for looking at battering in the historical context of patriarchal marriage:

> The use of physical force against wives should be
> seen as an attempt on the part of the husband to bring
> about a desired state of affairs. It is primarily purposeful
> behavior and not the action of deviant or unusual fami-
> lies . . . . Rather, men who assault their wives are actual-
> ly living up to cultural prescriptions that are cherished
> in Western society—aggressiveness, male dominance,
> and female subordination—and they are using physical
> force as a means to enforcing that dominance.
>   . . . The essence of the context specific approach is
> that the social world can be understood only by explor-
> ing human behavior in the settings in which it occurs.[2]

Sociologist Mildred Pagelow used quantitative methods
similar to those of Straus, Gelles and Steinmetz, but went
beyond their model, asking women about the patterns of violence, what they did about it and why they stayed. She focused
on the institutional responses to battered women who ask for
help and concluded that "People who find themselves in a violent domestic situation cannot, totally and by themselves,
either create or alter the situation in a vacuum. Much of their
response depends on the social and cultural environment within which they live. If we wish to address alternatives, we should
also examine forces that tend to prevent, block, or obscure alternatives."[3]

Like Pagelow, psychologist Lenore Walker used a model of
social learning theory and searched for explanations of why
battered women are often unable to see alternatives while they
are still enmeshed in the relationship. She pointed out that
many women who have been isolated and randomly punished
by violent men initially try everything they can think of to
change the situation. At first, they may have some success in
minimizing or postponing the violence, but as the relationship
continues, even this moderate degree of control diminishes.
Using M. Seligman's theory of "learned helplessness,"[4] Walker
described its development in battering relationships in this
way:

1. Repeated batterings . . . diminish the woman's moti-
   vation to respond. She becomes passive.
2. She does not believe her response will result in a
   favorable outcome, whether or not it might.
3. Having generalized her helplessness, [she] does not
   believe anything she does will alter any outcome.[5]

The woman eventually gives up trying. While to an outside observer it might look as if battered women could either defend themselves or leave, they have learned to be afraid and to believe that no matter what they do, nothing will bring about change.

The concept of learned helplessness has been useful in helping shelter workers and others understand "why women stay," and it sometimes helps women diminish their feelings of guilt or failure for staying with brutal men. Some feminists have criticized its seeming implication that women who are battered are generally helpless, but Walker's recent publications make clear that not all battered women move into the third step of helplessness. Many battered women are far from helpless in conducting aspects of their lives not related to the men who batter them.[6]

It seems almost a truism, by now, that many women who approached institutional representatives for assistance learned that they couldn't rely on help from anyone to stop the battering, or even for ending the relationship. When appeals to ministers, psychiatrists, police and prosecutors were of no avail, they eventually gave up trying to change their lives.

In recent years, it has become clear that changes in professional attitudes and the development of institutional willingness and capabilities have helped battered women leave violent men. However, we still don't know much about why some women left even after they had learned to be helpless, even when they had to do it all by themselves. One study indicates that *hopefulness about change* is a major motivating force for women to stay and ultimately for those same women to leave. At some point these women give up hope that the man will change his behavior, and instead develop hope that they can create a safe or rewarding life outside the relationship.[7]

The Cycle of Violence

Walker also developed the theory of the cycle of violence. The cycle has three stages: 1) tension-building, 2) violent actions, and 3) honeymoon or loving contrition. Couples in which men are violent begin romantic relationships in a "honeymoon" period. Then tension begins to develop (stage 1), rising at an uneven rate, exploding into violence (stage 2), which is followed by a resumption of the loving contrition or "honeymoon" stage (stage 3). Eventually, the cycle begins again.

Walker found that there was evidence of a tension-building phase in 65 percent of the cases she studied, and evidence for

loving contrition in 58 percent of them. Over time, in a
particular relationship, the proportions changed, with an increase in the tension-building stage and a decrease in the loving
contrition or honeymoon stage in long relationships.[8] (Walker
has also found that some women leave violent partners after the
tension-building phases become too frequent and too long, and
loving contrition phases become rare or nonexistent. This may
be related to the development of hope in some women for a better life outside the relationship.[9])

Knowledge of the cycle of violence is useful for those who
work with battered women. It enhances understanding and re-
duces the frustration and anger felt when "rescues" don't work
out as planned. Therapists, group leaders and shelter workers
often see clients only in crisis; that is, in stages one or two of the
cycle. Thus they never even hear about the positive aspects of
the relationship, because when a woman is frightened or
wounded, she can hardly remember that there have been some
good times. Workers may find it hard to believe that the couple
share some loving moments, and they may be extremely upset
when a woman suddenly and without explanation returns to a
violent man or changes her mind about following through on
the carefully made plans to leave. The cycle of violence provides
a partial explanation.

Although most women recognize the cycle, as well as some
feelings of helplessness, it's important to realize that the new
theories developed by Walker and others are in the infancy
stage, and that none of them fit each woman equally. In addition, one must be careful to explain that the cycle theory does
not imply that the violent man cannot control his assaults. The
fact that a "tension" phase precedes violence doesn't imply that
the man must release his tension by violent action. Many men
assault in a conscious effort to control, and their assaults don't
necessarily stem from inner tension. In addition, the tension in
a man who batters may result from his realization that he's unable to control the woman. Many women believe the men who
batter cannot help themselves, so it's important to emphasize
that there are other ways of releasing tension that can be
learned.

Feminist Therapy

The new feminist theories of battering are part of a larger
body of feminist theory that has been developing within the in-
tellectual wings of the women's movement over the last two

decades. Feminist ideas gradually have affected all areas of life and study, including psychotherapy. Feminist criticism of traditional therapy began proliferating as it became clearer that the "experts" in those fields were as much prisoners of their times as the general population. Therapists, no less than others, assumed that mature, healthy men would be dominant, aggressive and decisive, and that mature, healthy women would be submissive, passive and dependent.[10] They didn't make the connection between those respective traits and the potential for male aggression and physical violence against women.

Many therapists had adopted a medical model. That is, clients (or "patients") who sought help were assumed to be sick and in need of treatment by the therapist. The clients' problems were generally not viewed as related to their societal role, nor to power differentials between women and men.

Feminist therapists, in contrast, developed a social analysis of mental health problems, concluding that women previously considered "sick" were often reacting in the most adaptive ways they could to oppressive social institutions, restrictive sex-roles or the abusive men in their lives. Feminist practitioners also began to develop models that minimized power differentials between therapist and client. This was accomplished in several ways, including explanations to the client of the methods and theories relied upon by the therapist and willingness to disclose information about personal values and lifestyles. Feminist therapists help women clients understand that many of their feelings and problems are the results of a social system that affects all women, rather than merely an individual problem or fault. At the same time, they encourage women to maximize their own power and expand their role as much as possible. Many feminist therapists favor group therapy as the best way to reach these goals.

It is beyond the scope of this book to discuss thoroughly the developing feminist theories about therapy, and their impact on other psychological theories and practice. However, feminist therapy has been particularly important in work with women who are abused and the men who abuse them, as one example will illustrate. At about the same time the shelter movement was developing, family therapy and systems theory, which favor involving in therapy as many members of a family or "system" as possible, were also becoming increasingly widespread. Many feminist therapists have insisted that couples therapy is inappropriate and even dangerous for women who have been battered, and that systems therapy may be especially damaging. Systems therapy, as well as other therapies, may be used for good or ill. However, the emphasis on interaction between people, rather than on individual responsibility for behavior, lends itself to a tendency to blame the victim.[11]

Although there are systems therapists who use the theory and still emphasize the responsibility of the person who batters for his actions,[12] many suggest that the victim is at least partially to blame, and that she may have to change in order for her violent partner to stop battering her. Even though there is token recognition for the perpetrator's moral responsibility, the emphasis is elsewhere. Feminist therapists have countered this perspective—as well as more traditional therapies that support victim blaming—by emphasizing that the person who uses violence or other types of abuse is responsible for that behavior. Equally important is the principle that the violent partner must change his behavior *first*, and then perhaps the system and the flaws of the nonviolent partner may fruitfully be addressed.[13]

Feminist therapists and workers in shelters have learned a great deal about the internal processes, sexual politics and events that contribute to a woman's decision to leave, stay with, or return to a violent man. Unfortunately, many of them lack the time or facilities for publishing what they know. The movement against woman battering is less than a decade old, so it should not surprise us that the work of academicians and feminist therapists has barely begun to be integrated with the expertise of front-line shelter workers. It is our hope that in the next decade all of these groups will work together, enriching each other's thought and actions.

Notes

1. See Murray A. Straus, Richard J. Gelles and Suzanne K. Steinmetz, *Behind Closed Doors: Violence in the American Family* (New York: Anchor Press/Doubleday, 1980).

2. R. Emerson Dobash and Russell Dobash, *Violence Against Wives: A Case Against the Patriarchy* (New York: Free Press/Macmillan, 1979), pp. 23–24 and p. 30.

3. Mildred Daley Pagelow, *Women-Battering: Victims and their Experiences* (Beverly Hills, CA: Sage Publications, 1981), p. 47.

4. Martin E. R. Seligman, *Helplessness* (W. H. Freeman & Co., 1975).

5. Lenore E. Walker, *The Battered Woman* (New York: Harper & Row, 1979), pp. 49–50.

6. Lenore E. Walker, "The Battered Woman Syndrome Study: Results and Discussion," in *Representing Battered Women: The Role of Domestic Violence in Self-Defense, Custody and Tort Cases* (Seattle: Northwest Women's Law Center, 1984), p. 8.

7. Beverly Wigen Gravdal, "Battered Women: Learned Helplessness or Learned Hopefulness in Abusive Relationships," paper delivered at Association of Women in Psychology (AWP) Conference, Seattle, WA, 1983.

8. Lenore E. Walker, "Victimology and the Psychological Perspectives of Battered Women," *Victimology: An International Journal*, Vol. 8, 1983, Numbers 1–2, pp. 82–104.

9. Gravdal, op. cit.

10. I. K. Broverman, et al., "Sex Role Stereotyping and Clinical Judgements of Mental Health," *Journal of Consulting and Clinical Psychology*, 34, January 1970.

11. The following statements appear in one paragraph, written by Seymour L. Halleck, an advocate of systems theory: "There is ample evidence that family victimization is often a problem of systems, that all elements of the system or all family members play a role in its development (Halleck, 1978). Such evidence, of course, does not provide moral justification for the actions of child abusers or wife beaters. It does suggest that all elements of causation have to be considered in any process of treatment . . . Some wives provoke violence . . . Positive changes in the offender's behavior are more likely to be sustained if they are accompanied by complementary changes in the behavior of other family members. . . ." See his article "Vengeance and Victimization," in *Victimology: An International Journal*, Vol. 5, 1980, Numbers 2–4, p. 104.

12. Jean Giles-Sims, *Wife Battering: A Systems Theory Approach* (New York: The Guilford Press, 1983).

13. Anne L. Ganley, *Court-Mandated Counseling for Men Who Batter: A Three-Day Workshop for Mental Health Professionals* (Washington, D.C.: Center for Women Policy Studies, 1981).

Chapter 3

The Emergence of
Groups for
Abused Women

The Self-Help Movement

Women who have been battered follow a long line of others
who organized to help themselves and each other cope with
problems that were not adequately addressed by established social agencies. Since Alcoholics Anonymous (AA) began in 1935,
self-help groups of many sorts have grown and gradually been
given more credence by professional therapists and researchers. True self-help groups like AA are leaderless, and AA is un-
doubtedly the most widespread and successful of its kind.

Alfred H. Katz and Eugene I. Bender, co-authors of *The
Strength Within Us*, explained that the self-help movement began as a response to the "depersonalization and dehumaniza-
tion of institutions and social life; feelings of alienation and
powerlessness; the sense, for many people, that they are unable
to control the events that shape their lives; the loss of choices;
feelings of being trapped by impersonal forces; the decline of
the sense of community, or identity."[1] For women who have
been battered, abused and isolated, these are often not just feelings, but the facts of their lives.

Katz and Bender defined self-help groups this way:

> Self-help groups are voluntary, small group struc-
> tures for mutual aid and the accomplishment of a spe-
> cial purpose. They are usually formed by peers who
> have come together for mutual assistance in satisfying a
> common need, overcoming a common handicap or life-
> disrupting problem, and bringing about desired social
> and/or personal change. The initiators and members of
> such groups perceive that their needs are not, or cannot
> be, met by or through existing social institutions. Self-

24

help groups emphasize face-to-face social interactions and the assumption of personal responsibility by members. They often provide material assistance, as well as emotional support; they are frequently "cause"-oriented, and promulgate an ideology or values through which members may attain an enhanced sense of personal identity.[2]

A significant feature of self-help groups is "their spontaneous origin," said Katz and Bender, and if professionals do initiate the effort to gather potential members together, they soon minimize their activity or disappear altogether. Although many organizations designed to help battered women have begun in a spontaneous way, problem-solving or mutual-support groups have typically been started by one or two workers (professional therapists, grassroots activists, crisis-line workers) who perceived a need and then recruited members—usually after much publicity, referrals from professionals and other agencies, and a great deal of patient waiting for sufficient attendance to even call the gathering a group. In recent years professionals have offered groups through YWCAs or mental health centers.

Mutual-Help Groups for Battered Women

Women have found support and understanding from each other in many kinds of groups during the last two decades: consciousness-raising (C-R) feminist groups, displaced homemakers' and assertion training classes, groups for single mothers and AA groups specifically for women. Individual women who feel stigmatized, isolated, powerless and to blame for their problems benefit greatly from exchanging information and expressing feelings with others in similar situations, and women who have been battered especially so. Many women are fearful of their own power and have little experience acting in a nonauthoritarian structure, so the presence of leaders to provide structure and guidance enhances a sense of safety and enables each woman to take as much responsibility for the group as she is willing or able. This is the model we call "mutual help," in contrast to self-help groups that have no leaders or rotate leadership among the members.[3]

The impetus for mutual help for battered women springs directly from feminist ideas: women are the best experts on their own lives; women are often safer in relying on others who are like themselves than in placing their fate in the hands of authority figures; in speaking honestly to each other, women teach each other that their problems aren't merely individual, but are social, political and shared by many others; institutionalized sex-roles are damaging to women, and the first step in changing them is to understand them; individual women have power and collectively their power can be great; the best place for women to look for emotional support and practical help is often from other women.

In deciding how to respond to the violent men in their lives, women must make harrowing decisions with inadequate knowledge of the potential outcome of each consideration. This is a lonely task, and one in which family members and friends may play an influential role, whether supporting traditional roles and actions acceptable in the community, or encouraging actions that are different from what the community would approve.

Unfortunately, the friends or relatives potentially most valuable to a woman who has been abused may insist she leave the man before she is ready; may disregard her fears and loyalty and concern for the man; may, explicitly or by innuendo, blame the woman and exhort her to stay with the man, try to do her part better, or to keep the marriage together at all costs. Worse, the battered woman may be subjected to conflicting advice from different family members or friends. Or she may have called on the same people for help so many times that they are "burned out" and reluctant to rescue her one more time.

Women who finally do decide to make changes may call on the police or go to a shelter for assistance. But some may not be desperate or decisive enough to go to a shelter and many will want advice and information before turning to the police. A mutual-help group of women who are, or have been, experiencing similar abuse can become a woman's family, her friends and her advisors for the crisis period. For some members, the group continues to serve these vital functions long after the crisis is over.

A group enables women to reduce their isolation and feelings of being different, abnormal, at fault, crazy, etc. In addition, other women who have begun to change their lives are impressive models of how changes can be made, and they provide advice about how to get help from agencies. In the most active of groups the women act as advocates for each other, trade services such as childcare and some even become involved in the anti-battering movement.

Although some groups, such as the one we describe in this book, have clearly designated leaders, there is still a great deal of emphasis on group members helping each other. They can provide an atmosphere of acceptance, of community and, occasionally, even of laughter and fun that no individual counselor can duplicate.

All-Women Groups

These groups are composed entirely of women, including the leaders, and that is important. The absence of men frees women to express feelings and thoughts that they might inhibit in a mixed group. This may be especially true for a woman who has been abused and has learned to fear men and tell them whatever she thinks they want to hear. If battered women are to gain from the experience of a mutual-help group, they must learn to trust again and to risk intimacy with others. There is some evidence that members of all-women groups achieve intimacy more quickly than participants in mixed or all-male groups.[4]

Feminist Groups

Words like "feminist" and "consciousness-raising" are not often used by group leaders to describe what is happening in the group. Labels aren't necessary and may be misleading or threatening to some participants. When women get together and speak honestly about their experiences, their consciousness *is* raised. That is, they realize that their problems are not so much unique issues as they are examples of the collective problems faced by *women*. Individuals must still resolve their own situations, but by observing that other women have suffered similarly and have changed their lives, they gain hope. It's an additional advantage that women who've solved the same pressing problems are sitting right across the table as resources.

Although our group model was not planned with specific reference to the consciousness-raising groups, it shares some of the same purposes and principles:

Consciousness-Raising Group[5]

A. Issues: Participants' resistance to consciousness of oppression:
   1. Glorification of oppressor
   2. Excusing/feeling sorry for him
   3. Romantic fantasies
   4. "An adequate personal solution"
   5. Self-blame

B. Recognizing reasons for repressing awareness of oppression:
   1. Reasons for repressing
      a. Fear of having wasted past
      b. Fear of future despair
   2. Analyzing validity of fear
   3. Discussing women's struggles in context of history and of groups and movements

C. Consciousness expansion
   1. Personal recognition and testimony
   2. Going around the room with key questions
   3. Relating/generalizing

Mutual-Help Group for Battered Women

A. Issues: Participants' resistance to awareness of abuse:
   1. Attribution of power to the violent partner
   2. Excusing/feeling sorry for him
   3. Romantic fantasies
   4. Belief woman can change abuser
   5. Self-blame

B. Understanding the problem, recognizing the patterns of denial and protection of the abuser:
   1. Reasons for denial
      a. Fear of having wasted past
      b. Fear of future despair
   2. Analyzing validity of fear
   3. Discussing abuse of women in historical and social context and battered women's movement

C. Consciousness expansion
   1. Sharing secrets, recognizing each others' similar experiences
   2. Going around the room with key questions and doing exercises that illustrate common experiences
   3. Discussing brainwashing, Cycle of Violence, etc.

How Groups Help

Women who've been abused often express feelings of guilt or shame because they continue to love the men who abuse them. They blame themselves, or they may have been blamed by friends, family members or counselors. They often fear they will be criticized by anyone they tell about their lives. The weight of that apprehension is removed when they begin talking with other women who have had similar experiences.

Once a woman recognizes that she is not alone, need not be ashamed and is not crazy, she begins to stop blaming herself for the violence against her. As she shifts her focus from herself as the one at fault, she is able to look for the real cause of the violence. When she realizes her partner's violence is the most immediate problem, she may be ready to face her options in dealing with it.

Groups help women face the reality of what has happened to them, what might happen and what their responsibilities are to themselves, their children and their partners. They present an opportunity to explore options previously denied them. Groups provide a format for making decisions, and other participants' support bolsters their courage to follow through on them.

At any point in this process, a woman may get a glimpse of the truth to come, the potential for life changes and new responsibilities. As she begins to break through her denial, she may get a hint of the fearful options and become frightened back into an earlier stage of denial. This is a risk each person takes in coming to the group, and a woman who feels too threatened by the unknown may decide not to come back to the group because of it. However, it may help her take action later on.

In groups, women learn how to cope with difficult and new feelings. Many women have learned to deny most of their feelings in order to endure emotional and physical abuse with the least amount of pain. Once they begin to reexperience fear, anger, grief, loneliness or guilt, they may feel overwhelmed, unless they have the help of people who've experienced something similar. Other group members and leaders can help them recognize the feelings, respect the range of emotions as important, valid and "normal," and to explore or change specific feelings, if that is what the woman wants.

Women who are considering ending a relationship or breaking up a household face many practical problems. Some women may have been isolated and controlled for so long that they have lost the capacity to accomplish everyday maintenance tasks such as the ability to pay bills and buy necessary household items. Less familiar tasks, such as finding jobs and adequate daycare, often seem insurmountable. In addition, many women who are leaving abusive relationships must concern themselves with their own safety, with children who are violent or frightened and with building social networks to help them with information and support. Women in mutual-help groups often play the roles of mother, friend, advisor and advocate for each other during the period of transition, as well as occasionally providing transportation and other practical help.

As women who've been abused recover their health and learn how to take care of their lives, they gain additional strength from helping other women who are new to the group. The new women, who are still in crisis, marvel at how much the "old hands" in the group have done and how much they've learned, which gives the "old hands" the perspective they need to keep working at changing their lives.

Notes

1. Alfred H. Katz and Eugene I. Bender, *The Strength in Us: Self-Help Groups in the Modern World* (New York: New Viewpoints [Franklin Watts], 1976). p. 3.

2. Ibid., p. 9.

3. In her book *Outrageous Acts and Everyday Rebellions*, Gloria Steinem states that "networking is becoming to this decade what consciousness-raising was to the last. It's a primary way women discover that we are not crazy, the system is. We also discover that mutual-support groups can create change where the most courageous individual woman could not." (New York: Holt Rinehart and Winston, 1983), p. 197.

4. Beverly Hartung Hagen, "Managing Conflict in All-Women Groups," in Beth Glover Reed and Charles D. Garvin, eds., *Groupwork with Women/Groupwork with Men: An Overview of Gender Issues in Social Groupwork Practice, Social Work with Groups*, Volume 6, Numbers 3/4 (New York: Haworth Press, 1983), p. 97.

5. Adapted from Robin Morgan, ed., *Sisterhood is Powerful: An Anthology of Writings from the Women's Liberation Movement.* (New York: Random House, 1970), pp. xiii–xxiv.

Part Two

Getting Started

Chapter 4

How to Begin a Community Group

Assessing the Need

The past ten years of study and experience have revealed that physical and emotional violence is present in all communities: in rural areas and cities, cutting across ethnic, religious and class differences. While there is a need for continuing research about the abuse of women, there is no longer a need to justify the formation of a group for survivors of battering in your community. As a community organizer or prospective group leader, you may find the following organizational strategies useful.

One way to begin the process of community education and involvement in the issues of battering is to survey other human service providers regarding the incidence of domestic violence reported to them. Depending on the size of your community, your own time limitations, and whether you are acting as an individual, as a member of a team or as an agency staff member, you may want to interview community leaders and service workers in person. Where personal contact isn't possible you may want to send out a survey to key service providers, including police, public assistance staff, lawyers, prosecutors, mental health workers and clergy. Be sure you are including agencies who serve a diverse population. Ask them to record for a month the number of victims of domestic violence who request services. (You will need to provide them with clear definitions of the physical and emotional abuse that make up the general category of domestic violence.) Also, ask the respondents to estimate how many of these abused women they would have referred to your group had it been available. In this way you will encourage the workers to begin identifying battered women, to think about referring them to you and to become more aware of the problem.

The information you gather will give you a very rough idea of how many women may be referred to your group and a good idea of which community workers to contact personally on a regular basis for referrals. *It will not give you any idea at all of how many women will actually attend the group meetings.* We emphasize this because our experience has been that leaders often have unrealistic expectations when beginning a new group. Awareness of the large numbers of women who could benefit from the group, plus enthusiasm about referring women to it on the part of a few alert workers who see many battered women, often lead to unrealistically high hopes about the number of women who will actually appear at the first meetings. This can result in some unnecessary frustration for the group leaders, a problem we'll return to in the section on what to do while waiting for the group to begin in Chapter 6.

Sponsorship

Sponsorship of your group by a well-established organization can be a great help in starting and maintaining a group. The organization can offer a range of support: It may provide its own staff as group leaders, payment for leaders outside the organization, training for leaders chosen by a grassroots community group, or it may supply a meeting place, support staff and materials for publicity.

A sponsoring organization or agency with adequate staff can also offer emotional support to group leaders. This is especially important when the group is beginning and few women are attending, or when special problems arise.

Organizational support can give you the credibility you need among agency workers who will make referrals to the group. When discussing sponsorship with an agency, be sure to spell out your responsibilities and obligations to each other. For example, you will need to clarify who will oversee publicity and the work of group workers and childcare workers. If the agency's style or attitude toward "professionalism," or the policies of the board of directors conflict with your politics or what you see as the needs of the women, keep looking until you find a more compatible organizational home for the group.

Paraprofessionals and Professionals

The roles of professionally trained therapists who have graduate degrees in the "helping" professions, and of paraprofessionals or nonprofessionals who have no such degree, have continually shifted since the battered women's movement began. These roles remain as diverse as the domestic violence programs themselves, and it helps to understand their historical roots.

In some areas, grassroots women who've worked long, hard hours to put together a program have been threatened by the seeming ease with which professionals can "take over." Professionals have often been given important positions on a board of directors or have been hired as executive directors, and may have come to dominate the membership of a collective.

Because many shelters begin with inadequate staffing and funding, shelters may not be administered in the most efficient way. Workers have learned to live with imperfect organization reasonably well so long as outsiders don't view them with a critical eye. Professionals, who are accustomed to stable funding and traditional agency organization, may criticize collective procedures, or chronic experimentation with structure and organization, as being unnecessarily chaotic.

Some nonprofessionals and paraprofessionals view all professionals as part of the traditional systems that have damaged the women they're trying to help. If they're not familiar with professional theory or jargon, they may feel resentful of those who use it. Some won't ask for explanations to be given in plain English because beneath the resentment is fear of not understanding a professional theory because of inadequate training. Or, they may not examine a potentially useful idea because of anger or intimidation. With good will, as professionals and nonprofessionals work more together they will each become clearer about what they want to learn from each other and what they already know enough about to reject.

Professionals who are otherwise aware of the failings of their disciplines may still be defensive in the face of criticism by paraprofessionals. They may also feel guilty and thus accept responsibility for inadequacies actually reflecting social views over which they have no control. If professionals become defensive for these reasons, they may react with impatient criticism to nonprofessional ways of interacting with abused women.

As grassroots agencies become larger or better established and receive funding from agencies that require accountability, they often become more professionalized. Some workers view the changes as co-optation, others as greater efficiency. Conflicts between the two viewpoints sometimes cause a splitting off into separate organizations; other times they may result in a melding of creative energy so that the organization benefits from the best attributes of professional training and paraprofessional training, while suffering from few negative aspects of either.

Conflict between these two groups within a community is often covert and can result in the loss of valuable expertise from all. For example, in some cities an agency may be staffed by professional therapists who only as a last resort refer women to shelters or groups run by nonprofessionals. Or, when professionals and nonprofessionals meet, they may end up talking to the *image* each has of the other, rather than exploring and exchanging ideas and values. In the best of all worlds, professionally trained workers and paraprofessional workers meet and plan together, teach each other what they know and appreciate each other's special skills, attitudes and areas of expertise.

Professionals have learned to recognize and treat a wide range of serious and not-so-serious problems and to help people gain insight into internal and interpersonal dynamics. They also have learned techniques of helping people modify their behavior, thoughts and feelings. Paraprofessionals, at least if they're part of a feminist organization, understand the politics of battering, have learned to understand the battered woman's feelings of being trapped, how to cope with fear and danger, and to find resources to solve housing, public assistance and legal problems. Since they have not been trained to keep a professional distance, paraprofessionals sometimes can gain a battered woman's trust and confidence more easily than a professional therapist can.

Distance between a professional and her client is created in many ways: by subtle or overt reminders of status differences (e.g., the professional is addressed by last name and title, the client by first name); by probing areas of the client's personal life while disclosing nothing about the professional's personal life; by presenting agency demands, such as filling out lengthy intake forms, in which some questions may seem to have nothing to do with the problem; and by use of formal or stilted language, or professional jargon ("Your husband's behaviors indicate a lack of impulse control") rather than a style and vocabulary similar to the client's ("He didn't want to control himself, so he beat you").

Paraprofessionals who have not been trained to inhibit natural, empathic, intimate ways of listening to people's problems tend to approach others from a position of equal status, disclose similar reactions or problems in their own lives and speak in a more common language style and vocabulary. They may touch, hold a crying woman, listen to and talk to her for several hours, and accompany her as an advocate to meet with professionals.

It may be easier for a paraprofessional than for a professionally trained worker to keep a focus on the political and social issues important to an understanding of battering and to convey to abused women that they are victims of sexist institutions, as well as an individual abusive relationship.

On the other hand, there *are* important interpersonal dynamics at work in a group for abused women and important dynamics within each participant. A paraprofessional may miss the complex interplay between these dynamics or be confused about their significance. Or she may not know how to act in a useful way because she lacks a working conceptualization of all these issues. If there are seriously disturbed women in the group, she may not realize the seriousness of their problems.

The people who select group leaders should be explicit about their priorities and criteria. Armed with this knowledge and understanding the politics of battering, they should interview all applicants who meet their criteria, whether they are professionals or paraprofessionals.

Formerly Abused Women as Leaders

There are many advantages in having a group leader who has been battered but has successfully left that relationship. A formerly abused woman can bring empathy and a commonality of experience that enriches the group, and she can serve as a role model to the other women. However, there are certain potential disadvantages that should also be considered. If a leader has only recently escaped a violent man, the group experience may reactivate her fears or distort her view of the other women's problems, whether she is a paraprofessional or a professional. A leader who's been abused may also tend to think other women's situations are more like her own than is actually the case and may give advice based on her own experience, rather than helping each woman make her own decisions.

Some important considerations for hiring a formerly

abused woman as a leader might include the following:

1. How long has she been separated from the abusive man?
2. Does she have any ongoing contact with him (for example, child visitation)? How does this contact affect her?
3. Does she still seem emotionally or physically attached to the man or the relationship in any way, including the following:
   a. Is she still mourning the relationship or the dream of what that relationship might have been?
   b. Is she still fearful of the abusive man?
   c. Does she feel, or seem to be, addicted to that relationship? If so, what are the effects on her, and on her relationships with others in her life now? How might these relationships affect her ability to lead the group?
4. Does she seem angry or impatient with women still in abusive relationships?
5. How aware is she of the many forms that abusive relationships can take? Does she seem aware that her experience will vary in many ways from that of other women, even though they may share many important experiences and feelings?

Ultimately, those making hiring decisions will need to carefully evaluate the circumstance of each candidate. The benefits of hiring a formerly abused woman can be many. However, if the woman is not thoroughly disengaged from the relationship, her own ongoing struggle to free herself might easily rob her of the considerable strength required for group leadership.

Other Leadership Issues

Every leader must have an understanding of, and training in, the politics of battering. That is, she must fully realize that battering is a social problem, a problem that persists because of the power differential between men and women. This is so, even though lesbians, gay men and other family members may also be violent toward each other. The complex forces that lead to violence are exacerbated in heterosexual couples by a number of factors: gender differences in economic power and social status, the nuclear family structure, romantic tradition, and role expectations promoted by social institutions.

If the social aspects of battering are not understood, leaders may do more harm than good to women in relationships with violent men. They may, unwittingly or purposefully, give the message that the woman asks for and deserves a violent partner, and that message will compound the problems of guilt and self-blame the woman may already have in abundance.

Experience in counseling, or in giving direct aid or referrals to women in trouble or under stress, is an important skill for leaders. This need not be "professional" experience, but it will be an advantage if the work was done either under supervision or with a more experienced colleague, or in a structured learning situation. Some examples of useful experiences would include working on a crisis phone line, as a shelter volunteer or as a rape relief advocate. The potential leader should be asked to describe what she learned, what was difficult for her and skills that need improvement.

Group experience is extremely important. If the prospective leader has conducted a group, she'll be able to say what she found easy and difficult about it. Training can then be arranged to provide additional skills she may need. Experience in group leadership that is similar to a group for battered women (such as leading a group for incest or rape survivors) is the most desirable training. If no one in your own organization is qualified to lead the group, keep an open mind about professional versus paraprofessional, and look for understanding, warmth, experience and openness to learning new skills. One professional and one paraprofessional leader, or one leader who has been battered and one who hasn't, often work as a good balance.

We recommend co-leadership of groups for abused women, and we'll return to this issue in Chapter 6. We feel that it is helpful for co-leaders to be similar enough in perspective to work well together, but different enough in lifestyle, age or ethnicity to enable a broad range of women to identify with them. Make an effort to ensure that at least one co-leader is a woman of color. Her presence will become known in the community, and other women of color, especially of the same ethnic group, will feel encouraged to attend the group. They'll also feel more comfortable in the group and more confident that their specific situations will be understood.[1]

Notes

1. Little has been published for or about women of color in abusive relationships. However, two books forthcoming from The Seal Press in 1985 will partially fill that gap: *Mejor Sola Que Mal Acompañada: Para la Mujer Golpeada/For the Latina in an Abusive Relationship* by Myrna M. Zambrano, and *Chain Chain Change: For Black Women Dealing with Physical and Emotional Abuse* by Evelyn C. White. For information write to Seal Press, 3131 Western Ave., #410, Seattle, WA 98121.

Chapter 5

Organizing Your Group: Issues and Alternatives

Safety and Confidentiality

A community group for abused women is never completely secret for very long, and you will have to decide, on the basis of the size and population of your community, whether there's any point at all in trying to keep the location unknown to most people. Maximum safety of group members is the most obvious reason for trying to ensure secrecy. If the man who has assaulted a woman knows she's going to a group for battered women, he will feel threatened and may want to "counterattack." If he can easily find the group, he can lie in wait for her or even disrupt the group, frightening the woman he's after and the other group members as well.

In the small rural community where one of us conducted an abused women's group in her private office, a group member was harassed each meeting by the abuser. While she was in the meeting he would leave "love" notes or hate notes in or on the car she drove to the group. Finding these notes after each meeting was upsetting and frightening for her, and for other group members as well. After a few months of meeting in this location, another abuser obtained the phone number of the office and called during each group meeting. He never identified himself, nor spoke. One of the group members felt sure it was her abusive husband from whom she was separated. She stopped coming to the group in an effort to protect the other members, despite the group's encouragement to keep coming. The calls stopped. Clearly, the danger faced by many of the women who attend the group must not be minimized or denied.

In the urban setting where we have conducted groups for eight years, there have been only a few instances of an abuser coming to our meeting place to cause trouble. Group members or leaders have never incurred any violence in connection with taking part in the group. However, we're aware that this could happen at any time. We may have experienced little difficulty because our group meets on the second floor of a large public building that houses only women and has a desk clerk on duty at all times. We know of other groups and leaders who have been threatened by the presence of a menacing husband or boyfriend, sometimes with weapons. We are also aware that individual women have suffered reprisals from abusers for choosing to go to a group, as they do for participating in many other kinds of activities.

Privacy

A second reason for secrecy of location is for the woman's privacy. In a small community, if a certain buildng or office becomes known as the place where battered women meet, women may be reluctant to enter it, feeling that just walking in the door places a label on them. Many communities have found that the best way to get around this problem is to hold the group meetings at a well-known public place, like a YWCA or church or community center, where people enter for diverse purposes.

The group meeting time and room number can be posted along with other activities but be called a "Women's Group," "Rap Group," "Support Group" or any other general name. Greater secrecy can be maintained if it isn't posted at all, but some privacy can be maintained by enabling a woman to find the room number without having to ask for the "Battered Women's Group." If there is someone at a reception desk, she or he can be informed of the character of the group. Take time to sensitize the receptionist to the feelings of the women who must ask for the group but who may not want to call it by name.

Location and Accessibility

The experience of coming to a group for the first time is itself frightening and will create some anxiety for most women. True accessibility maximizes the chances that all women are able to come to the group without experiencing extreme fear or discomfort beyond that inherent in their personal situations. Providing accessibility involves paying careful attention to the provision of childcare, the physical accessibility to the building

and meeting room by disabled women, the character and population of the neighborhood, available transportation, as well as
the safety and privacy measures discussed above.

When deciding on a location for the group to meet, look for a
place that is in a busy area of town, that is well-lighted, near
public transportation if possible, or even close to a police sta-
tion. In some situations, the best place may be in the shelter for
battered women, but of course if that location is secret from the
public and you have half a dozen new women coming to it every
week, your security won't last long.

We are aware that in some communities there is no public
transportation, there is no lighting on the streets, and the police
may be more of a danger than a help. The solutions to these limitations will come, as they have in each community that begins a
shelter or group, from your intimate knowledge of the
strengths and weaknesses of your own community and your
personal resources. They'll come from brainstorming, being in-
ventive and courageous, and from learning from your mistakes.

Although almost any location is likely to discourage some
ethnic, economic or age groups from venturing to it, you can
minimize this problem by locating the group in a central place,
either downtown or in a service center used by every segment of
the population. When you are thinking of a location, go there at
the hour you are planning to have the group meet and make a
visual check to see if there are many young or older women
using nearby facilities. Note how many unattached men are in
the area and whether there is a mix of ethnic and racial groups.
It may seem—or even be—central. But if only white people feel
comfortable enough to go there, if only middle-class and physically able people who have cars can easily get there, if after dark
it seems too threatening for any women except those who have
no choice, then it's not really what we would call accessible.

The character of the room in which you meet also makes a
difference. Try to provide a warm, comfortable atmosphere
with home-like furniture and some bright, cheerful colors. The
reality is you'll probably have some worn and lumpy sofas, and
perhaps a few chairs with questionable underpinnings. Or you
may have secured a nice new well-lighted room that has board
room furniture and seems extremely cold. Make the most of
what you have available, as these problems are probably the
least important of many you'll face.

It's the style—even a principle—in some women's groups to
put large pillows on the floor and sit in close circles of sister-

hood. There may be value in that for some groups, but this seating arrangement is not appropriate for groups of battered women. Since the group reflects society at large, some of the group participants will be older or disabled. These women, and any who are suffering injuries, will not feel comfortable sitting on the floor. If you provide chairs for these "exceptions," everyone will probably feel uncomfortable sitting at different levels. In addition, many women who have for the first time worked up their courage to go to the group will want to find something that seems not too different from what they are used to. Neutral-seeming physical surroundings will help participants relax sufficiently to hear the messages of the group, which may sound quite unfamiliar, even radical, at first.

Ideally, every group would provide wheelchair accessibility and an interpreter for the deaf. These issues are rather like the childcare ones to be discussed in the next section, in that they are of greater ethical and political importance than is reflected in the actual number of women affected directly. It may be extremely difficult to provide a deaf interpreter or wheelchair accessibility. Then, when you've gone to a lot of trouble or expense to find a building with a ramp entrance and to hire an interpreter, months will go by before anyone indicates a need for either one. Yet if you compromise in the beginning, you're likely to find it even more difficult to make demands for what you need later from possible funding agencies.

Whatever compromises you decide are necessary at the beginning, try to look ahead to when you will be able to add services or better access. Try to locate in a building that has room for children. If the building doesn't have a ramp, see if it can be included in the future construction plans. Or choose a place that has an inside elevator and few outside stairs so that you can improvise a low ramp, when appropriate. Your group will flourish in a much more stable way if you can keep it in one building for a period of years so that your referral sources and the general population of women know they can count on it as a steady resource over time. When a woman does finally gain the courage to go to a group, a wrong address or the necessity to make an extra round of telephone calls because workers aren't sure just where the group meets that month may be all she needs to give up.

Organizing Childcare

Even though some group participants don't have children or can make other provisions for them, many women cannot go anywhere unless they can take their children with them. This is so important that we're tempted to advise not starting a group at all until you can guarantee reliable childcare. Once you start without childcare, you may be unwittingly giving the message that providing childcare is not so important after all. This will make it even more difficult to acquire childcare later on. But if you're operating on a shoestring, you may need to follow the well-tried feminist principle of doing whatever you can, however inadequately, because you're the only ones who are going to do it, and it's better to do it the best way you can than no way at all.

Our own experience has been that it is difficult to conduct a group meeting with a child in the room, even a sleeping infant. The effect of the child's presence can be either inhibitory or disruptive, making it difficult for the group members to give each other the attention and support they need. (However, other groups report that they have been able to incorporate children into meetings.) If for some reason childcare is not available, or a mother has difficulty leaving her young child with the volunteer, we may say to her: "We want you to have an opportunity to focus on your own needs and concerns. So that you and the other women can have the attention you each deserve, we'd like you to (depending on circumstances) . . . let your child go with the volunteer and trust her to call you if necessary; take turns with other mothers in the group looking after the children in the childcare room, since our volunteer hasn't come tonight; or if absolutely necessary, find alternative childcare arrangements that you're comfortable with and come back next week."

Providing childcare is no simple matter. It means acquiring a second room, not too far from the group room, but far enough away so that mothers can't be distracted by the voices of their children. The room should be soundproofed or far enough from other adult activities to reduce the likelihood of complaints about the normal noise of children. It means collecting toys and educational or creative supplies for activities that lend themselves to imaginative, educational and nurturing care for children of all ages and cultures, including some children who are extremely fearful, aggressive or shy. Ideal childcare workers would be knowledgeable, reliable, consistent and sensitized to cultural differences and the special reactions of children who have lived with a violent parent. A well-established sponsoring agency may be able to pay them for their services. Low pay is preferable to none, since it provides future leverage with funding agencies for increasing pay.

It is very important to teach childcare workers the various effects of parental violence on children. This education could be provided by shelter workers or other available community experts. Stress the advantages and limitations of how much the workers can help in a two-hour session. Teach them their obligations and options if they have reason to think a child is being abused. In addition, childcare workers should be sensitized to the childrearing customs of the cultural groups they are likely to encounter. This is no easy job, and you're unlikely to find qualified people for it unless you pay for their expertise.

In addition to all this, you will never know, in a drop-in group, how many children to expect. Ideally you will have two childcare workers on tap at all times, because even one unhappy baby plus one active two-year-old can be too much for one adult. Three easy three-year-olds plus one wild one can mean that the well-behaved children are once more ignored, playing ultraquietly in the corner that seems the safest, just as they do in their frightening homes. On the other hand, your two faithful childcare workers may have only one happy ten-year-old to care for, week after week. Or weeks may go by with no children to care for, and as soon as you let one childcare worker go, the next week you'll have seven children, all under four years old.

This situation is very similar to the problem for group leaders starting a new group who have few or sometimes no women in attendance. It's even worse perhaps for the childcare workers, who may have a sense that all the action is in the group and that they're wasting their time. If they're volunteers, they may suffer a great drop in morale and stop coming. If they're paid, your funding agency may soon refuse to continue paying them. Two partial solutions to this dilemma are: 1) to promote the childcare job as an educational one, and 2) to invite the childcare workers to sit in on the group when there are no children or to take turns sitting in when there is only one child. (If absolutely necessary, you might agree to pay them only for the time they are caring for children.) They will gain a better understanding of the children by listening to the mothers and will not feel they are wasting their time.

If you can find a student in child psychology or a related field, she may find the experience is payment enough, since she will have a special opportunity to learn about the effects of violence on children. An advantage of the childcare worker sitting in on the group may be that some mothers, reluctant to leave their children with strangers, will feel secure enough as they get to know the woman to leave them in her care. (Sitting in means participating in group discussions and exercises enough to be a part of the group, rather than a mere observer.) Also, the children may gain more from being with the childcare worker than they would by being left at home with a babysitter who has no special knowledge of the family situation.

Some groups have found that nonsexist men's service organizations are willing to provide nurturing, specially trained men to do childcare, and this can be a special benefit for children who have never spent time with a non-violent male. (This opinion is shared by two of the co-authors; the third prefers only female childcare workers to provide services in this group setting.) All childcare workers and the children's parents should understand that under no circumstances is any kind of physical punishment allowed, nor will violence be permitted among the children.

Fees

Assess your own financial resources and develop a policy you can live with. Since many abused women have little, if any, money, try to provide the group at no cost to participants. Interestingly enough, one recent study[1] found that clients in psychotherapy who did not pay a fee for service reported lower levels of symptom and problem distress than did clients who had paid for service.

The Drop-In Format

The most predictable aspect of these groups is that each week the number of participants will change, as will their personality, race, class and lifestyle. The unpredictability of the group stems mainly from its "drop-in" character. That is, a woman may attend without any prior screening and without commitment to attend more than one meeting. This model, in which each woman determines what is best for *her* regarding her attendance at the group, suggests right at the start that she can be in control of her decisions and actions.

Many women will attend only once. Often they will have received what they were seeking: specific information, confirmation of their perceptions of their relationships, or a simple "testing of the waters" to reach out for help. It is impossible to predict who will return a second time or who will become a "regular" for a time. Some women attend regularly for an initial period of several weeks and return sporadically for support (often at holiday or anniversary times) or when they've experienced further abuse, harassment or threats. A few women may attend for as long as three to six months. A very few might return on an occasional basis for a year or more.

A core group may form within the drop-in structure, and may remain intact for a month or more. These women develop a mutual bond and return regularly to renew their contacts, catch up on news of each other and exchange emotional support. Four or five core group members may occasionally form car pools to come to the group and may meet socially outside scheduled meeting times. They may also provide practical help to each other, such as trading childcare or accompanying each other to difficult interviews with lawyers and welfare workers.

Occasionally, for short periods, only the core group may attend the group meetings. This will provide an opportunity to explore topics and issues in greater depth than is possible when most members are new or in crisis. Core group women are likely to request referrals to additional or alternative women's groups or to counselors as an extension of their positive experiences in the drop-in group. If a "second phase group" (see Chapter 11) exists in your community, you may want to present this as an option to participants after a period of regular group attendance and when initial crises seem past. Try to stress that they have the final choice over which group they'll attend. Otherwise, they may feel you are "kicking them out" of the group. The choice is always theirs.

Groups in Shelters

You may choose to have a mutual-help support group within a shelter, and if the location is secret, you might decide to limit it to shelter residents or take the risk of opening it to ex-residents. Some non-secret shelters make their groups available to community women, whether they've stayed in the shelter or not.

In nearly all respects shelter groups can be organized on the same principles as the community group we describe in this book. However, since crisis counseling, referrals and information will often have been provided in one-to-one sessions at the shelters, you may have more flexibility for exercises and topics that are appropriate for groups in which participants know each other and are not in crisis.

In a shelter-based group there will be times when you may experience the benefits of having a relatively predictable attendance. At other periods, however, the turnover may be so great that your group in the shelter will resemble a drop-in community group. In either case, you will recognize in the shelter group significant differences from a community group, as well as many similarities. For example, in a shelter group there may be special problems that grow out of the intimacy and intensity of group living. Conflict or tension among very aggressive or passive women forced to cooperate in the daily tasks of living may tempt you to turn the mutual-support group into a house meeting. Try to resist. Avoid issues such as who left the greasy pan in the sink, and, if necessary, say that the next house meeting is the best place to resolve specific problems among residents. Explain that the exercises you do in the group will make it easier to deal with such problems. The personal interaction issues that commonly arise in shelters can be used to enhance an understanding of abusiveness or passive and aggressive behavior, and can also provide opportunities for women to practice communication skills, assertiveness, anger control and expressing their feelings.

As you gain experience in leading shelter-based groups, you'll become familiar with their special character and may need to adapt the material we present in this book. If your groups are mandatory for residents, for instance, you'll need to keep a balance between flexibility and consistent expectations. If children are present, you may have problems in getting them off to the childcare room or to bed. Because the women will often be spending much time together outside of group, your beginning and ending rituals for the group may be different. You also may be able to provide much more follow-through than is possible in most drop-in groups. Use your imagination to modify and build on the ideas we suggest here.

Notes

1. Carol Yokes and Jeffrey Berman, "Does Paying a Fee for Psychotherapy Alter the Effectiveness of Treatment?" in *Journal of Consulting and Clinical Psychology*, Vol. 52, No. 2, 1984, pp. 254–260.

Chapter 6

On Being A Group Leader

Getting Started

For support and for strengthening your skills, it's important to consult with people experienced in both group counseling and in work with battered women. Ask them for help as you prepare to lead a group, and for their assistance as continuing resources. If there is an organization of people working in the area of battering, joining it will provide an important source of information and support. If not, you might want to think about starting such a network. Look for organizations at the national, state, city and county levels, joining each, if possible, and building a strong, supportive network for yourself. This is especially important if you are geographically isolated from other people doing this kind of work. Reach out now, before burnout has a chance to set in. (See the list of resources included in the bibliography at the back of this book.)

Waiting for the Group to Begin

Once the leaders are chosen and publicity is out, everyone associated with starting the group may then be stunned by the lack of response. You should be prepared for somewhere between a few weeks and many months of waiting in an empty or nearly empty room. Three women may attend the first meeting, one the next, then nobody or six and then nobody. No one need blame herself. It will probably take a while for agencies to remember the group and for word of mouth to get to battered women, who will then need to gather the courage to show up.

It can be discouraging for group leaders to sit in an empty room, but it won't be so bad if you can work on publicity while you're waiting. Or use the time for sharing information with your co-leader about your expectations for the group, new books, or other group experiences. Working as a volunteer group leader for a group that is slow starting can be particularly demoralizing. But there are special problems in being a paid leader when there's no group going. You may have to deal with the disapproval of the funding agency, who may even decide after a few weeks that the group was not a viable idea after all. If that occurs, do everything you can to persuade them to wait six months, at least, before giving it up. During that testing time, you might decide to take turns being leader, rather than both of you being paid for your time.

If it seems absolutely necessary, one option is postponing hiring a special childcare worker. When the need for childcare arises, you can take turns (with one of you leading the group and the other caring for the children) until you have a stable enough group to predict the need for childcare. This is, however, far from ideal and should be seen as an emergency option only.

Even more difficult to handle than a total lack of participants is the attendance of just one woman. You've offered her a group, and where is it? If two leaders are present you can become a group of three. This is one of the situations in which it's a distinct advantage to have leaders who have been through the experience of battering. If neither you nor your co-leader have had this experience—or if you don't have a co-leader—you may have to improvise. For example, if a particular woman you've met at a shelter or among your friends has been battered and come through the experience feeling strong, you might ask her to come to the following meeting. Or have her call the woman in the "group"—with the other's permission, of course. (See Chapter 11 on "The Group of Two.") Be honest with the woman about the difficulties of beginning the group. Remember, this is not an individual counseling session and shouldn't be conducted as such, since the woman came expecting to be part of a group.

Co-Leadership

Defining Your Roles

Realizing that you may face limitations in terms of finances or availability, we nevertheless strongly recommend co-leadership of drop-in groups for abused women. We've discussed some of the issues related to selecting a co-leader, and the need to develop and maintain a strong support network, an important member of which is your co-leader. Now you will want to consider another dimension to the issue of co-leadership, that is, the use of power.

Sharing the power of leadership can present a strong model to women in the group by showing that mutual respect and support are attainable goals in a close relationship. After all, co-leading a group for abused women requires a commitment to an intense and intimate working relationship. You will spend at least three hours a week together, planning, working and relaxing. Group members notice the interactions of the leaders and are sensitive to disruptions in the relationship. Relaxed and friendly exchanges, verbal and non-verbal, between the leaders create an atmosphere of safety and trust in which the group can function well.

To minimize confusion and misunderstandings during group meetings, decide on a structure for sharing responsibility. You may want to consider rotating the primary leadership role on a weekly basis. In this arrangement, the primary leader for the week decides (usually in advance) on the *content* of the meeting, i.e., what topic or exercise she will focus on in the meeting. She is also the one who might completely change or abandon this plan, based on her assessment of the individual members' needs and the composition of the particular group. The primary leader is concerned also with timing in a group session, with balancing the needs of the individual members with those of the group as a whole and with the more mundane tasks (such as taking a break and starting and ending activities).

The co-leader, in such a division of responsibility, would be concerned more specifically with the *process* of the group. She would concentrate her attention on the responses of the individual members to the topic or exercise. She can help move things along by offering comments if the tempo is lagging, or she might help to calm an agitated woman. She might choose to intervene if she feels a group member is experiencing difficulty, or she might simply cue the primary leader by eye contact or a word of concern to notice a particular member. The co-leader often has more attention available to see or hear an individual group member's strengths or difficulties and to make supportive comments or gestures, while the primary leader in the meantime is encouraging group interaction and cohesion. (For a description of another co-leadership model, see Susan Hartman's article in *Social Work with Groups*.[1])

Communication and Mutual Support

If the two leaders have worked together for some time, they may feel comfortable discussing differences in point of view or approaches during the group. While such disagreements may prove ultimately positive, the potentially negative effects for some group members must be considered carefully. On the one hand, presenting two valid viewpoints that diverge illustrates the kind of "argument" an abused woman may well experience within herself. Thus, to hear it outside, between others, may enable her to realize that she is dealing with complex issues for which there are no simple answers.

On the other hand, some women may be frightened by such disagreements, mild or "theoretical" as they may be. Any sign of conflict may remind a group member of the danger and abuse she has experienced in response to any form of disagreement with her partner. The group leaders must always be sensitive to the special concerns of women who have experienced violent, physical retaliation (as well as emotional abuse) for what would be considered "normal" discussion and dialogue in other relationships. Leaders can take the opportunity to describe what they're doing to allay participants' anxiety. "We're disagreeing, but notice that we're not angry." Or, "I'm a little irritated, but it doesn't have to turn into rage or hurt anyone. When you've been in an abusive relationship for a while, it's easy to forget that other ways of relating are possible."

Before and after each session, it's important to check with your co-leader to see how each of you is feeling about yourself and about the group. For example, before the meeting you might confide, "I'm feeling quite excited about the group tonight. I've had a fine day and feel rested and ready to go. I hope we can continue some of the topics that came up last week, if any of those same members return tonight." Or, "I'm feeling extremely tired. I hope that Joanna doesn't return and try to dominate tonight, like it seemed to me she did last week. Do you have any ideas how to cope with that if it happens?" Or, "I'm feeling personally very sad about the loss of a friendship. But I think I'll feel energized when group starts. Let me know at the break, or even during group, if you think I'm projecting any of my own sadness onto the group members."

Together you can also try to identify any external stressors that could be modified to make life easier in the group, such as room temperature, environmental noise, or the set-up of tables and chairs. Remind each other that you have limited influence and no control over the decisions that participants make for their lives. Years of social conditioning won't be erased by just the one right word or exercise; change is an ongoing process.

Evaluation

Reviewing Your Goals

If you know what you want to gain from the experience of leading a group, you're much more likely to get it. Think right now about why you want to be doing this work. What do you hope to learn? Is it in keeping with your political values? Does it fit into your career plans in some way? Do you have any idea of how long you'd like to be leading a group? Write these thoughts down, as specifically as possible.

After you've been leading the group for two or three months, think about whether you're getting what you wanted or accomplishing what you'd hoped. Read through your original list of goals and write down a preliminary response to them. Could any changes in the set-up of the group bring you closer to your goals? It might be useful to discuss any dissatisfactions with your co-leader now, even if you can't imagine a way to change things. Brainstorm. Two heads are often more productive than one. And remember that you will feel more skilled with more experience. You could set some new goals for yourself if the original ones are easily being met. Discuss these with your co-leader, your supervisor if you have one, and with your colleagues. Review these goals again each three months and don't forget to give yourself credit for doing a hard job.

Feedback From Others

You might want to develop an evaluation form that is given to women at the end of group each week, month or when a participant thinks it's her last session. Some useful questions might include:

1. How was this group helpful to you?
2. What aspect of this group was not helpful? How could it be improved?
3. Would you refer other women to this group? Why or why not?

Perhaps you could leave time at the end of sessions to review what went well and what might have left people feeling uncomfortable. There are no rules about this kind of evaluation; find what works for you and your co-leader.

If you are being supervised by or working with a more experienced colleague, it can be helpful to plan a joint evaluation or consultation after three or six months. Don't forget to affirm the things you do well or are learning to do well, as well as those that need work. Describe what you do well in addition to the things you'd like to change or the skills you'd like to gain.

It is also important to meet with your co-leader after the group to evaluate the session and plan for the next one. Give each other compliments for the specifics you liked in an evening, as well as for each other's overall assistance. A useful format is for each of you to say what you did well in the group, and only after you've complimented yourself to say what you would like to have changed. Beginning with self-evaluation and with the positive makes it much easier to go on to the next step of saying what you think the other did well, and then what you would like to see her do differently.

If you don't want criticism after the session because you're too tired, or feel stretched too thin, ask your co-leader to make a note of the criticism for a later time. Look for ways in which your approaches might be different and try to view them as complementary, rather than becoming competitive about which is correct or works better. Remember that evaluation is part of building mutual support, which will help you to develop and strengthen your skills as a group leader.

Notes

1. Susan Hartman, "A Self-Help Group for Women in Abusive Relationships," in Beth Glover Reed and Charles D. Garvin, eds., *Groupwork with Women/Groupwork with Men: An Overview of Gender Issues in Social Groupwork Practice, Social Work with Groups: A Journal of Community and Clinical Practice,* Volume 6, Nos. 3/4 (New York: Haworth Press, 1983), p. 133.

Part Three

Leading the Group

Chapter 7

Structuring the Flow Of the Group

Welcome to the Group

Preparing for each group meeting may require a great amount of patience and flexibility on your part. The room in which your group is always scheduled to meet may have been painted just a few hours before; the childcare worker called in with the flu; and you realize that you've run out of the required agency reporting forms. It's at times like these that you and your co-leader give each other a small smile and plunge into the hard work of helping this gathering of women become a group.

The beginning of a group session is rarely neat or orderly. All of the activities of settling in, which include filling out forms by members and helping mothers get their children to the childcare room, are important in setting the tone for the meeting. Flexibility is important initially, as women are likely to straggle in, no matter what the announced starting time.

The following outline will give you some suggestions on how to structure the weekly group meetings.

Assembling the group and completing forms	20 minutes
Introduction and formal beginning	5 minutes
Brags	10 minutes
Activity (Topic, Exercise)	35 minutes
Break	10 minutes
Activity	30 minutes

Ending
    phone numbers
    safety check
	10 minutes

Total group time	2 hours

Maintaining a regular structure from week to week enables returning members to have an increasing sense of comfort and security. As with other aspects of leading the group, you will need to remain flexible in maintaining a structure that fits the needs of your group and your leadership style.

As new and returning members arrive, the leaders set out on the tables hotline or crisis information cards, brochures and pamphlets on legal issues and resources, emergency shelters, medical and financial resources, and fliers on current groups and events of general interest. Copies of local papers or national magazines with recent news stories about abuse are often brought in by returning members. All of the informational material may be taken by the group participants, preferably at no cost.

You might also find it useful to print a brief "Welcome to the Group" handout to give each member, which explains the basics of the meeting day and hours and gives the emergency 24-hour phone numbers of shelters and crisis lines.

Forms

If your group receives public funds, it's likely there will be some reporting requirements for financial accountability. In addition, public funding sources (as well as private) are interested in obtaining statistical information that will assist them in justifying the expenditure of funds and in evaluating future requests for continued funding.

Client confidentiality is compromised by reporting requirements, regardless of how carefully and thoughtfully the forms are designed. It's important to make it clear to the group participants that they are welcome in the group whether they complete the forms or not, and to acknowledge that many women find the forms intrusive, irrelevant, and sometimes incomprehensible. It is up to each woman to choose how much she will reveal about herself.

Returning group members often are glad to assist new women with the forms. If many women find the questions about physical and emotional abuse very upsetting, you may want to use the form as a topic for group discussion.

Participants have sometimes asked us to sign a form for another agency verifying that they have attended the group. Since we disagree on this, we each do what makes sense to us. We don't always agree, either, on whether we should cooperate with lawyers who want us to sign affidavits or offer testimony for an individual group member. One of us believes it is imperative to refuse in order to safeguard the use of the group for the sole benefit of its membership. The other two believe legal action may be essential to help some women, and it need not threaten the group. Each situation should be judged individually on its merits. As a group leader, you can anticipate such requests and develop a policy that is in line with your values and political views.

Introduction

A formal introduction to the group meeting helps focus the individual's attention on the beginning of the group experience. Returning members who may have been exchanging news and gossip with each other will be brought into the group as a whole at this time. You might begin with a few sentences such as:

"Welcome to the group. My name is Karen and I'm one of the leaders. Sandra is the other leader. This is a group for women who have been in or are now in an abusive relationship.

"We're here every Wednesday night, and we meet from seven to nine p.m. We'll be taking a break around ten past eight. For those of you who enjoy smoking, please feel free to smoke in the lounge or restroom at break time."

As you explain the basic structure and ground rules of the meeting, your relaxed and calm tone will help relieve some of the initial anxiety the participants are experiencing. New people find it very comforting to know that they will not be put on the spot and that they may participate as fully as they want to without fear of being put down or humiliated.

Leader: "Our first concern in this group is for the safety of each of the members. For this reason we ask you not to discuss personal information or stories you hear during the meeting outside of this place. This could put others in danger."

Most women react positively to this message. Connecting the issues of confidentiality and safety at the beginning helps the women to know that their safety is a priority issue, and it offers them a model for putting this first in their lives.

In addition, as part of your introduction, you will need to make a statement about your policy on reporting child abuse or neglect. It's important for the group members to know that there are some instances in which the laws of your state and your policies limit certain aspects of their confidential relationship with you.

As part of your concern for confidentiality you may also want to suggest that group members use their first names only.

Brags

Good for rape group

Leader: "We like to start each group meeting by asking each person to say briefly something you feel good about having done this week, or in the past few days. Try to think of one thing, large or small, you've done that has given you pleasure or helped you gain more control over your life. Please say your first name and then your short brag."

In order to set a tone that will help new people know what is being asked of them, encourage a returning member to volunteer to begin the brags. She will be able to illustrate that brags are very brief, for example:

"I made it here tonight!"

"I bought myself a new blouse today."

"I made it to work every day this week."

"I didn't call him all week."

"I left my husband yesterday."

"I looked for an apartment."

A woman in crisis who has come to the group for the first time may begin to tell her story of abuse the first time she's called on to talk, for example, during brags. Just speaking in front of the group may cause her such anxiety that she has difficulty limiting what she says. You will need to exercise great tact in helping her to shorten her story and allow others to tell their brags. There's no "right way" to accomplish this, and it's one of the most difficult parts of the leader's job.

You might try reminding her:

Leader: "We're just telling brags now, Janet. We'd like to hear more about your situation in a little while after everyone has had a chance to give their brag. Thanks."

Brags serve several purposes, as you can point out: "Taking credit for what you've done well and reminding yourself it's all right to do things for yourself can be the first step in raising your self-esteem. Women who have heard little but criticism and insults from an intimate partner for months or years have usually begun to criticize and insult themselves, and this is a good time to reverse the process."

Leaders participate with their own brags, and often provide

an opportunity for the other women in the group to see that all of us sometimes have trouble thinking of positive things to say about ourselves. One of the co-authors chose to give up smoking during the time she co-led the group. This decision became a brag that she used almost every week for a long period of time. Those group members who returned for some time took pleasure in sharing the leader's struggle with an addiction, and compared it with their struggle to stay away from an abusive relationship. Each week of remaining free from the destructive effects of an addiction is a shared victory for those who have stopped smoking or using other drugs or for those who didn't answer the abuser's calls or letters.

Choosing the Activity

After hearing the brags of each woman and the responses of the group members, you'll have a good idea of what activity will be most helpful with this particular group. You may have learned that a woman is in extreme crisis, or that all of the participants at this meeting have left their abusive partners, or that there are several women who are so needy they will use as much group time as is offered. The choice of activity will depend on this kind of information, as well as on what you have already prepared to do. If there are many returning members, you may even be able to carry over a topic begun in previous weeks.

There are three types of group activities that can be used alone or in combination during a group meeting: Topics, Exercises, and Individual Time. As a general rule, the more cohesive and well-functioning the group participants are, individually and collectively, the less structured the activity needs to be. On the other hand, if the group members appear fragile or frightened, and if the issues they are facing currently are dissimilar from each others', then the group will need a lot of structure and help from the leader.

The less cohesive group, which would benefit most from a structured activity, might include a woman in crisis, a woman who has difficulty speaking because of a disability, two women who want to continue to believe their husbands will change, two women who left their abusive partners six months ago and are wanting to discuss dating problems, and a woman who is withdrawn and appears to be seriously disturbed. While this may sound like an improbable combination, it is not unlikely that you will encounter such a group if you have a drop-in format.

For this group, a structured meeting that will provide concrete information and support will be most useful, at least to begin with.

Topics

In general, topics are the best choice when there are more than eight participants and their needs are diverse. A topic focuses the attention of the group members on a common theme and provides a sense of coming together for a shared purpose. A topic also provides a way for women to tell important parts of their stories and offers the leader a means of setting limits by keeping group members on the topic. Another advantage of the topic format is that even though each woman cannot focus on her individual problem, everyone will be able to talk some.

Starting with a topic and then changing to individual time after break can offer a good balance for some group meetings.

A slight variation on offering a topic that you've preplanned is to ask the group members what topics or issues they would like to discuss or gain some information about. For instance, women may respond by asking, "How do I tell my children why they can't see daddy?" "What do I tell my boss when my husband harasses me at work?" Or, a woman may say, "I don't know how to talk to my parents about what's happened to me." After everyone who wishes to contribute has described her idea, you might draw together common themes and ask members to focus their discussion on those common areas, such as assertiveness, the continuing tendency to deny and to protect the violent partner, equating disclosure of the partner's violence with self-blame, or finding personal and economic support.

Exercises

Group exercises may be the most appropriate choice of activity when there are about eight women participating, most of whom have attended the group at least once before. Some exercises that are primarily educational in focus seem to work well with any size group. The "Cycle of Violence" exercise (see Chapter 10) is a good example of an educational exercise. It is handy to have several of these general, educational, structured kinds of exercises available to choose from for any group session.

A small group of women, most of whom have been to the group meetings before, will be able to enjoy more intimate and participatory exercises such as "Visualization" or "Saying No."

Most of the exercises described in Chapter 10 will take up one entire group activity time of thirty minutes *plus* an additional thirty minutes for discussion. Thus, it may not be possible to combine the more complex exercises (including some of the "brief exercises") with another type of activity such as a topic or individual time.

One of the pleasures of leading a group is creating and leading exercises that are interesting, informative and helpful to the group participants. A few guidelines to remember are: keep the exercise simple, straightforward and nonpressuring. A group member should not feel put on the spot or "pushed into" participating. If she chooses not to participate, she needs to be helped to remain connected with the group. Perhaps there's a way she can assist you by passing out paper or some other activity that will help her to continue to be part of the meeting. Sometimes a woman may feel content just to remain in good eye contact with the leader while she "rests" in the safety of the group meeting. Usually, if a woman realizes that her decision not to participate will be honored, she will feel safe enough to try to join in. Only on very rare occasions has a group member chosen not to participate in the exercises described in this book.

Individual Time

It is most useful to begin by offering to hear individual questions or stories in the following situations: 1) when the group is small (fewer than eight women), 2) when there are a majority of returning members, or 3) when there is at least one but fewer than four individual women in crisis who need the immediate attention and support of the group.

You may want to switch from discussion of a topic to providing time for individual women to talk at more length during the second half of the group, after the participants are more comfortable with each other and can appreciate the limitations of the group more fully.

In either case, whether before or after the break, you will want to find a way of dividing the time available (approximately thirty minutes) among the women who have indicated a need to talk. It's useful to remind the group members of the time frame: "We'll spend the next half hour discussing individual concerns . . ." Then, you might ask each member how much time she would like, or you can leave it open to the members to be aware that they are sharing a very limited amount of time. It's also helpful to remind the group of realistic limitations: "It just won't be possible for everyone here to have individual time since it would mean that there would only be three minutes per person, so some of you will need to wait for a turn next week. But if you're in a critical situation, it's important to speak up now, so that you do get time."

Ask a woman describing her individual problems what kind of feedback she would like from the group, or whether she just wants to talk and then hear that others are understanding and feeling for her. Women who have never been in a group and who have learned to suppress saying what they want often lose sight of knowing what they want. If you keep presenting participants with the opportunity to think about what they want, it encourages them to understand that they really can decide what they want from the group and that they can ask for it.

Remember, however, it remains an important part of the leader's job to take primary responsibility for setting the limits for each member's use of the group time. It takes practice and discipline to lead the group in their use of individual time, to help the group process to take place and to add information to what members have to share. If you think that you have "the perfect solution" to a woman's problem, or a good idea about a resource to explore, wait. See if others are willing to talk. If they aren't, ask, "Has anyone else ever felt like that? Faced that problem? What did you do? How did it work out?" After others have spoken, you can give your ideas as well, if they haven't already been mentioned.

A major and difficult task for group leaders is to maintain your awareness of quiet group members while you're engaged in a particular participant's description of her situation. The co-leader can take special responsibility for noticing whether group members are listening or whether they've emotionally left the group. Victims of abuse have often learned to "tune out" painful experiences and observations; therefore it's especially important to provide maximum opportunity for group interaction, so that members can be fully present to give and receive support.

At times it may be necessary to interrupt the flow of a woman's story in order to reengage the attention of the group. Each leader might say, "You're talking about a lot of extremely painful things that have happened to you, and I'm sure other group members are feeling for you as well as remembering their own pain." And then, "Would you like to hear from them?" Or, "Would you like to hear some ideas about how you might reduce your pain?" Or you could say, "You're expressing a lot of anger/ sorrow/anxiety. I'd like to take a moment to see how the group's reacting and then we'll get back to you." However you deal with it, just interrupting the flow of the woman's story will break some of the tension and focus attention in the *group*. Just be sure you get back to her.

Scheduling a Break

A five- or ten-minute break taken halfway through the meeting allows women to smoke outside of the group room, buy refreshments from a vending machine or—most importantly— talk in small groups or pairs. Break time can be the most important part of the group session. The informal contacts that occur during the break often change the tone of the meeting dramatically, so that when the group reassembles, the leaders may need to readjust quickly to a deeper level of trust or to an increased willingness to address new issues. Often the break serves as a convenient time to shift from a topic or exercise format to an "individual time" format.

Break time also offers an opportunity for the leaders to consult together about group progress, to plan for the remaining time or to decide how to handle an individual problem. At this time, individual women may want special attention; however, it's usually best to resist being drawn into long, one-to-one discussions. Most individual questions can be handled better during the group. Encourage the woman to bring up her concern, with your help, for the group to consider.

Ending the Meeting

It's very important to provide a definite end to the meeting, rather than to allow the participants to drift apart. If some members drift off one by one, those who are left and who are talking about important decisions and feelings may feel hurt or rejected, so we encourage you to use the same ending each meeting. Two useful closing activities are an exchange of phone numbers and a "safety check."

There are some groups, however, in which arriving late and drifting away at unpredictable times is not perceived as rejection. Leaders should discuss the question with participants and adapt their time schedules to the cultural milieu in which they're working. In some way, compromise must be reached between cultural groups who have very different views of time. And, of course, the needs of the co-leaders must be taken into account as well as those of the participants.

When suggesting that the group members exchange phone numbers with each other, hand out paper and pencils to those who need them to encourage the process. Emphasize that there are many reasons why a person might not want to give her number and that no explanations are necessary. On the other hand, you can also point out that many women come to the group feeling there is no one they can talk to about their lives. If they give and receive numbers, they'll go away knowing that there are quite a few people they can talk to during the week who will understand what they are experiencing and who will be able to listen empathically. In addition, ask each woman to state whether there are certain hours when she does not want to be called, and encourage the caller to ask if the other woman can talk. Remind the group it is important to give each other honest answers, rather than being "polite."

At the end of one of our group meetings one of the women told us apologetically that she could only be called from midnight until six a.m. at her work place. She felt sure that her number would be of no use to anyone, but she gave it willingly and said she was available to the other women at those times. Sure enough, in subsequent group meetings we learned that several women called her in the middle of the night when they were feeling most frightened and lonely and couldn't sleep. The woman at work also was glad to have the company on the phone of an acquaintance from the group.

(Some group leaders may prefer to encourage people to exchange phone numbers just after break as a way of reinforcing the informal, social contacts that often are initiated during the break.)

The end-of-the-group *safety check* affirms once again the leaders' concern with the well-being and safety of the members, and acknowledges the reality of the danger and fear that participants live with daily. It provides a model of recognizing the risks and at the same time offers a constructive means of responding to them. For example, ask if anyone needs a ride home with another group member or would like to be walked to her bus stop or car. This not only maximizes safety, and the feeling of safety, but also creates another opportunity for women to talk together in twos and threes, laying the groundwork for continuing relationships.

In addition, you may want to take these final few moments to review the shelter resources available in your community, and to encourage any woman who feels it is not safe to go home to consider going to a shelter instead.

Assure participants that the group will be meeting next week and you hope to see them then. You may need to follow up with a woman in crisis who needs help locating a shelter or crisis counselor, or you may want to make a note for someone of a referral resource for her to contact during the week. Most of the time it is possible to anticipate these situations and state to the woman in the presence of the whole group, "Let me tell you about that after the meeting," which provides a feeling of openness and avoids special attention to one group member.

At the end of most meetings, however, you will be tired and will need to have a little time (with your co-leader if you have one) to relax and to review the difficulties and pleasures you experienced during the group.

Chapter 8

Responding to Special Needs

Providing a group for abused women emphasizes the common strengths and needs of all the members. Therefore, it is not useful or productive to focus on the needs of only one group member to the exclusion of others, as though you are in an individual counseling session. Some problems presented by subgroups in a given meeting may divert you from the main task of promoting positive interaction among all of the members.

The following discussion is intended to provide you with an overview of the kinds of special problems that clusters of group members or individual participants may present during a meeting. As feminist theory suggests, however, it is important not to confuse a person with a label or problem category that refers only to a set of experiences in a person's life. As in all other aspects of working with abused women, it is crucial to remember the social and political context in which they are living and making choices for their lives. The group meeting itself is a social context that affects the decisions a woman will make about how she will engage, confront, embrace or otherwise participate with the other members and the leaders.

Handling Problems in Group Composition

In a group that is usually composed of women of a single race or ethnic group (including the leaders), women of another race and ethnicity who attend may hear or become the target of racist remarks. Such remarks are often made in indirect ways and most often are not consciously intended to personally attack another group member. They may, for example, take the form of thoughtless jokes that mock a racial or ethnic group.

Since these groups are designed for women in heterosexual

relationships, you might assume that participants are less likely to be offended by anti-lesbian or anti-gay remarks, and be tempted to let them go by. This is not necessarily so, and there may be someone in the group who is a lesbian or closely involved with someone gay or lesbian. Your obligation as leader is to protect the group from abusive language, and homophobic comments must never be condoned, in any case.

It is essential that offensive or stereotyping comments be dealt with immediately and honestly by leaders, regardless of the form they take, and regardless of the composition of the group. Your first response will be to make a clear statement that you feel the remark is hurtful or lacking in respect. If the group is small and there are many returning members, you may be able to encourage a group discussion of racism and homophobia and their relationship to sexism and abuse of women.

If the group is large and diverse, however, often the best you can do is to stop such remarks from continuing. It may feel awkward, but it's important that you take a direct leadership role. You might say: "Dorothy, I'm not sure you're aware that what you've just been saying about Native Americans might be offensive and hurtful to some members of the group."

If Dorothy continues, defensively, then you may have to be more forceful: "Dorothy, please stop now. Perhaps, Joan, you can go on with what you were saying about looking for work."

The effects of religious discrimination, such as anti-Semitism, can also cause severe distress for some members of the group, and it's important to recognize sensitive situations and take appropriate action. Offensive remarks, such as anti-Semitic jokes or phrases, must be dealt with firmly. Religious differences may surface in a number of other ways—for example, what may be commonplace language usage to one woman may be experienced as sacrilegious by another. Again, how you handle such differences will be determined to some degree by the composition of the group, but whether or not any particular group member is personally offended, the main issue for the leaders is to stop the abusive, stereotyping language.

Although many unusual situations may occur which you cannot plan for, we mention a few examples here so you can become aware of the kinds of issues you may need to face in your group and to think over how you might want to handle them. Even in a large, metropolitan area, women who have known each other before or who have mutual friends, ex-boyfriends or even abusers in common may find themselves face to face in a group meeting. Sometimes they are relieved or delighted to see each other, and at other times it's extremely awkward. The leader may need to facilitate a discussion between these women that will enable them to remain in the group, if they so choose, with some degree of comfort.

Another kind of conflict may occur between women who have left an abusive relationship and those women who remain with the abusive partner. Women of these two subgroups may view each other with some suspicion, fearing that the other will not understand or respect the decisions they've made to remain with or to leave the abuser. If you sense this is a problem, you can help by reassuring the group members as a whole that each woman's choice for her own life is respected in the group. It's also useful to remind group members who appear to be experiencing pressure from the differences among them that each woman is making personal decisions that are part of her process of change and growth. The concern of the group is for the safety and well-being of the members, and they can be encouraged to express their fears for each other, or their sadness, rather than criticizing others' decisions.

Mother-daughter pairs bring special needs and interests to a group meeting. Sometimes the mother will come in support of the daughter, and sometimes the daughter comes to assist the mother. There is always a great deal of tension in these pairs because the need to be accepted and understood is nowhere more intense than in this deeply intimate relationship. Either one may be afraid to speak openly of the abuse of father, husband or boyfriend. The overall atmosphere of tolerance and acceptance of the group greatly supports the attempts of mother and daughter to understand how the abuser has affected both of their lives.

In the group we co-led, three sisters attended together for three months. They used the group to forge a reunion and to build a new understanding and basis for their relationships. All three had experienced both physical and emotional abuse, and they struggled to overcome the myths, stereotypes and fears of intimate connection that had kept them isolated both from each other and from others whom they felt might not understand the pain of the abusive situations. The sisters became a group within the group, which was helpful to them for a short time, but eventually became limiting. For the leaders, it was a challenge to deal with these two "groups"—the group of sisters and the other participants—simultaneously.

Responding to the Needs of Individual Women

Multiple Problems

When an individual participant has a long history of deprivation and abuse, the most helpful strategy is first to clarify the issues she describes to the group. For example, she has run out of food; she has no money for a lawyer; Children's Protective Services has been called; she has started drinking again; her parents abuse her emotionally; her husband is an addict. The next step is to elicit from the group concrete suggestions of community resources that might be of some help to her. It's essential to keep the pace of the group moving by encouraging many members to share their ideas, or the group as a whole can quickly become overwhelmed by the seemingly endless list of unhappy and unresolved experiences in this one woman's life. The two most important messages you can give to the participants are that: 1) you acknowledge her problems as both real *and* capable of solution, and 2) she has taken an important step of reaching out to others by coming to the group. If, in addition, she chooses one suggestion to act on during the next week, she'll have a clear sense of beginning to control some aspects of her life. You can also refer her to other agencies, especially those with appropriate crisis lines.

Physical Injury

Women rarely come to a group meeting in need of immediate medical attention. However, you will see injuries such as black eyes, cuts that have been stitched and bandaged, bruises, painful stiffness, and a combination of physical and emotional shock. Don't assume that a woman has sought medical help. She may be too frightened or ashamed of her injuries. She will need to learn from you and others about a safe place to get the medical attention she needs, such as a women's clinic.

All group members need encouragement to take their health seriously. There are many kinds of "hidden injuries" of battering: broken ear drums, noses and ribs; hypertension; loss of sight in an eye; adhesions; and a multitude of gynecological problems. These injuries often go unmentioned, neglected, and are taken for granted until they are discussed in the group and identified as injuries.

You may find that some women tell the group about being beaten and hurt as though they have no feelings. They describe being choked, kicked or slapped in the same colorless tone that one might describe grocery shopping. This splitting off of one's feelings—such as pain, rage and fear—from the physical experience of the abuse is a psychological tool commonly used for coping with physical and emotional trauma. Often a woman will become aware that others are reacting more strongly to what she is saying than she is herself. This may cause her embarrassment and confusion. She may begin to feel isolated and "crazy" if she is not helped to understand what she is experiencing. For example, you might say, "Debra, it must have been very frightening to be held down on the bed and choked like that. Other women have told us that they 'tuned out,' or 'went away' or 'stopped feeling' when they were being hurt. I wonder if you have put your feelings aside for a while in order to protect yourself from being hurt any more."

This kind of statement from the leader can be very relieving to the individual woman and other group members. You can also encourage women to notice the caring and empathic responses of others in the group as they describe the very painful experiences they have had.

Emotional Shock

Women who have been severely abused, emotionally and/or physically, often describe and show a constellation of reactions that can be described as "emotional shock." When this term—shock—is mentioned to group participants to help describe what they appear to be experiencing, they respond with relief to know they they are not going "crazy" (as they had feared) and that there are things to do to help cope with emotional shock.

The symptoms of emotional shock that you may see or hear described by a woman include many of the following:

- confusion
- glazed expression or dazed look
- inability to focus on outside tasks or events and/or internal preoccupation
- inability to identify or talk about feelings
- startled reaction to noise, light, touch
- intense fear, often generalized
- exhaustion, fatigue, insomnia
- appearance of paleness, weakness, being underweight, often caused by poor nutrition

A woman in shock needs information about her experience

from the leaders and other participants. She needs help in understanding that her reaction of emotional shock is time-limited, and that it is a normal response to an abnormal event. She needs encouragement to take care of herself, which may mean relying on others for a safe place to stay and for some physical care. Encourage a woman in shock to be with others. Remind her that she should have the following: rest, proper nourishment, a sense of order and routine, people who can assist her with short-term decision making. Above all else she needs to be safe. Suggest that shelters and homes of relatives and friends are important resources to consider.

A woman in shock may find it almost impossible to fill out forms or to participate in the group discussion. Although she may appear to be focusing on the group topic, it is likely that she's not able to follow the discussion or activity. What is of greatest benefit to her is to experience a caring environment in which she is provided with information and understanding.

A woman can be forced back in to the state of shock even after she has separated from the abuser. For example, a woman who came to our group, having fled from another state, showed many of the symptoms of emotional shock described above. She continued to have symptoms of shock for several weeks. Slowly she regained her physical health, settled into permanent, safe housing, and her financial situation began to stabilize. She came to the group each week with new progress to report, and the regular members took delight and strength from her continued improvement. One night, however, she came to the group meeting dazed, exhausted, fearful and introverted. Immediately the group members recognized that she seemed the same as the first night she had come to the group. The regular group members and leaders gently explained to her that she appeared to be in emotional shock and asked what had happened to cause it. She described a telephone call she had received a few nights earlier in which the abuser had threatened to kill her and had also threatened the safety of her children. Reminding the woman about shock, helping her to realize that she had been retraumatized, and remembering with her that she had survived the previous period of shock helped her know how to best care for herself. Her recovery from this second episode of shock was more rapid than the first.

Serious Disturbance or Psychosis

The experience of emotional shock is not commonly understood as a possible result of physical and emotional violence. Personnel in emergency rooms, health clinics and agencies may mistakenly diagnose the symptoms of emotional shock as those of other mental health problems. For example, the woman who appears "out-of-touch" or preoccupied may be experiencing a temporary state of emotional shock, or she may actually be experiencing a break with reality that is more common in the psychotic process.

Another example is that of the woman who is extremely fearful. To those who do not understand the real dangers of battering, an abused woman's fears may seem excessive and without foundation in reality. She may be labelled "paranoid," which is just another way of discrediting the reality of the danger she is in. For some women, however, paranoia is an actual problem in differentiating real from unreal dangers. For the untrained worker and for the woman herself, this can be very confusing, since many women who have been abused have incorrectly labelled themselves "crazy"; that is, they are convinced that they have more serious mental health problems than they actually have. The amount and degree of abuse they've experienced may be so extreme as to be "unbelievable"—and unbelieved by professionals from whom they sought help—and yet it all really happened. Your belief and understanding can be the best way to reduce their feelings of "craziness."

For some women who are in great distress and who are experiencing a serious emotional disturbance, such as schizophrenia, the group can seem alienating and frightening. Or a woman who is experiencing the manic phase of a manic-depressive disorder may find herself talking too much in the group, taking over the group activity, unable to follow the group discussion but barging into it anyway. All of these actions cause her to feel even further out of touch with others, and her sense of isolation increases. She may then become angry, even belligerent, defending her behavior.

It is important not to permit this situation to escalate, which could increase both the participant's anger and fear and the group's aggression and insecurity. The group leader needs to take confident action in a calm and direct manner. If possible, the woman should be helped to remain in the group. You might need to say, "Celia, right now we're discussing Jane's question about her legal problems. Perhaps you have specific information that would be useful to her."

If Celia continues, instead, to talk excitedly about her jealous lover and "the other woman" and to be unaware of others in the group, then you may need to be more direct, asking her to just listen. However, if your interventions don't work, it may be necessary to help her to leave. Usually the best time to deal with this situation is at break time when co-leaders can consult with each other and the woman can be spoken to individually. She may be relieved and appreciate that you are aware of her distress and are willing to help her. Although openness is important in groups, there are times when an individual's feelings of safety and privacy take priority. *Leader*: "Joan, it seems that it's hard for you to follow the discussion in group, and that you have a lot that you would like to talk about. Perhaps you would be more comfortable talking one-to-one with a counselor." Affirm the woman's real need for assistance; after all, that's why she came to the group. Help her identify resources more appropriate to her present emotional state.

If your group meets in a facility where there is a woman counselor on duty at all times, such as a YWCA, the counselor may be able to talk right then with the group member who needs special attention. When the group reconvenes, explain that Joan is talking with the counselor downstairs so that she can have more individual time, or that she's gone home with her sister, or whatever the actual events are.

During the past several years, we have had to call for a hospital aid car to assist with a group member on only one occasion. At that time a group member was experiencing acute anxiety, nausea and severe headache. Since she was in such obvious pain and we had no way of determining what medical problems she might be having, we suggested she go to the hospital and she readily agreed.

Women who have been in abusive relationships have become accustomed to having their fears, illness, pain and suffering ignored, belittled or minimized. It can be a positive, though difficult, experience for the leader to directly confront the fact that a participant is very distressed and needs a different kind of help. We prefer this option to that of pretending that the problem doesn't exist, thereby allowing disruption of group trust and safety.

Another kind of emotional distress occurs when a woman is unable to follow what is going on in group primarily because her attention is focused on an internal world whose reality is more clear and present than that of the external, "real" world of the group. Her comments in the group just don't fit. For a while she may sound very intelligent, and then one gradually realizes that what she is saying doesn't make sense. There are few boundaries between her internal fantasy life and the outside life of people and events. It is helpful to speak quietly and directly to her, affirming that she is in a safe place. Acknowledge that her contributions to the group are valued, and that you will help each person have time to talk and to identify resources in the community to assist them.

"Wonder Woman"

Another group member who may present special needs that require a response by the leader is the "Wonder Woman" who appears to have boundless energy. Often she describes that she has "just left the *&%#!" and she is trying with every ounce of strength to begin a wholly new life *this instant.*" During the group meeting she dazzles the women with her accomplishments and often overwhelms them with her feats of cheeriness and enthusiasm.

This group member will need a lot of help with limit-setting and realistic goal-setting. She also will need the support of other group members who can help by describing the *process* of recovery they have experienced. She most especially needs to feel in contact with others, since a major component of the "Wonder Woman" persona is isolation: a feeling that "I can do it all myself—I have to!" Hopefully, you will find an opportunity to gently remind this woman:

"You are very exhilarated now, and you have really accomplished a lot this week in getting an apartment, signing up for school, applying for financial assistance and getting daycare for the children. I just want to remind you that you will need to rest and slow down a bit, which may seem to you like a big letdown. It's important to remember that this letdown is as 'normal' as the 'high' you now feel. Life may feel like a rollercoaster for a little while, even for several months, until you have a new routine established and some of the major emotional and physical changes you are now experiencing have decreased. Try to be patient with yourself."

It is often the air of confidence that Wonder Woman communicates that convinces her and others that she's not vulnerable to returning to the abusive partner. However, it is at this very time in the process of the separation that she is the most vulnerable to depression and to returning to him. The leader can ask if other women have experienced that sequence, and when the woman understands that she might experience a dramatic and negative change, she can guard against feelings of failure and the consequent vulnerability to returning to the violent partner.

Wonder Woman's denial of her fears of loneliness and of depression may cause conflict with other group members. In an effort to cope with her own feelings she may be insensitive to others. It is necessary for the group leader to respond to this kind of conflict among group members in a firm but gentle manner. You may want to say something like the following:

Leader: "Jane, because you have taken so many strong and courageous steps recently, it may be hard for you to remember how frightening it can be to leave the relationship, go to a shelter or to live on your own. This group is a safe place for each person to talk about the situation she is in without feeling criticized or put down. We'd like to move on now to hear from others in the group about how they are dealing with the problems we're discussing."

In an extreme situation, the leader might have to be more forceful. *Leader:* "Lydia, I am aware that you think I'm not understanding you just now. However, I must ask you to just listen for a while. It's important that each person here has an opportunity to talk."

Depression

Lost in the shadow of the Wonder Woman, that determined survivor, is the woman who is experiencing severe depression. Often this depression is related to the experience of living with extreme emotional and physical stress and deprivation for an extended period of time. Most abused women have experienced some degree of depression during the abusive relationship. Talking about grief, loss and sadness in the group meeting often helps women recognize their emotional experience and begin to plan activities to cope with the depression. Regular exercise, adequate sleep, nutritious meals and some enjoyable events to look forward to are essential. Equally important is to be with others, especially those who understand battering.

The *Diagnostic and Statistical Manual III* provides the following list of symptoms of this kind of depressive syndrome, stating that "during the depressive periods at least three of the following symptoms are present":

1. insomnia or hypersomnia
2. low energy level or chronic tiredness
3. feelings of inadequacy, loss of self-esteem, or self-deprecation
4. decreased effectiveness or productivity at school, work or home
5. decreased attention, concentration, or ability to think clearly
6. social withdrawal
7. loss of interest in or enjoyment of pleasurable activities
8. irritability or excessive anger (in children expressed toward parents or caretakers)
9. inability to respond with apparent pleasure to praise or rewards
10. less active or talkative than usual, or feels slowed down or restless
11. pessimistic attitude toward the future, brooding about past events, or feeling sorry for self
12. tearfulness or crying
13. recurrent thoughts of death or suicide

The authors share varying degrees of skepticism overall about the DSM III, but find this a useful, commonsense checklist of symptoms of depression.[1]

Loss and Grief

Another group member who is experiencing a great deal of emotional pain is the woman who has just separated from the abusive partner. Her depression results from the loss of her love partner, her home, her familiar surroundings, perhaps her children, her pets, her favorite chair, her clothes, her financial security, her companion, her lover. This woman typically sits quietly and stoically while activity goes on around her. She doesn't cry, since she is certain that others would think her silly for missing her cat, for having romantic thoughts about the abuser, or for wishing she had the favorite sweater she had to leave behind. Her grief is profound, and if not acknowledged it may drive her back to the abusive relationship as the "lesser of two evils"—loneliness and despair or battering.

The grieving woman experiences her loss and sadness as all-encompassing and endless. It is difficult for her to hear that other group members may have experienced a similar sadness and that they are now able to laugh as well as cry, to feel pain and gladness. It can be very helpful and important for the grieving woman to hear some information about grief and mourning. She feels much less frightened and lonely when she hears someone say: "It's very hard and painful to give up not only the person you cared about and your belongings, but also to give up *the dream* of what you had hoped this relationship could be, of the kind of life you hoped to have with this person."

Suicide

Sometimes a group participant does not seem to respond to others at all, and she is not able to benefit from talking about depression. She may mention thoughts of harming herself, or of "just going to sleep and forgetting it all—for good." Ask her directly if she is thinking of killing herself. How specific are her suicidal plans and images? Does she have the means to carry out these thoughts? Does she seem disconnected from her feelings, i.e., very cool, reasonable and calm about ending her life? Has she started giving away objects she treasures? Is she suddenly feeling "up," seeing the end of pain in sight via death? These are some of the warning signs that there is a very high risk of her following through with her suicidal thoughts.

The suicidal participant may respond well to suggestions from you to seek help, to enter a hospital voluntarily or to go to a mental health center. Also, you may have women attending the group meetings who have just come from the hospital or who are out on pass from a hospital where they are getting help with their suicidal feelings. It's important not to shy away from these very powerful and painful feelings and experiences, but to discuss them during the meeting in a supportive and caring manner. It enables others to let her known they value her life and encourages the participant to view herself more compassionately. In addition, each group member is given a message that her life is important. Participants are listened to empathically when they express doubt about their desire to live, especially those feelings of hopelessness. The leader also needs to be informed and to consider in advance her legal and ethical obligations to suicidal participants. Develop a general strategy ahead of time so that you can respond flexibly to a specific situation.

Silent Members

You may, from time to time, have one or more group members who say so little that you wonder if they're getting anything from the group. It's important not to put them on the spot by asking them to explain their silence or by centering attention on them. They may be depressed, or in shock, or shy, or just following their cultural norms. You can find out by talking to them in a nonpressuring way outside of the group.

A fairly nonthreatening way of encouraging them to open up is to have frequent opportunities for each member to respond to the same question, to say briefly how they feel or what they think.

Occasionally a woman may decide she thinks the questions asks something too private. Suggest that she try speaking her answer to herself silently, or try writing it down, since speaking and writing tend to clarify thoughts.

Fear

The legacy of fear often remains with a battered woman long after she has left the abusive partner. In the group she describes a daily life experience in which every moment and activity is filled with fear, the basis of which is the past abuse and/or the continuing, persistent harassment by the abuser. She feels that there is no escape from him. She is pursued in the home, on the job, by phone and by mail. Friends and relatives are also subject to the harassment. She receives candy, she gets threats: both kinds of contact engender fear. She is not safe!

This group member feels crazy; she calls herself "paranoid." She no longer trusts her own judgment or instincts. She feels, and often acts, helpless and paralyzed, unable

The expression of fear finds wide recognition within the group meeting. Other women vigorously nod their heads in agreement as one woman tells of always looking over her shoulder, expecting to see the abuser.

Convincing a participant to decrease her isolation and to recognize that there's "safety in numbers" is an important aspect of helping her with her feelings of fear. A woman's fear can be her best ally in staying safe if she can learn to use it in her own behalf. You may want to demonstrate a way of "reframing" a commonly described experience of fear by explaining, "When you look over your shoulder for the tenth time and are still frightened, remind yourself that there's a reason for 'watching out.' You're looking over your shoulder in order to protect yourself, and you're doing a good job of it. This may help you to be more patient and trusting of your feelings." Encourage the woman to talk to herself in that kind of affirming way, even as she's peeking through curtains or otherwise double-checking her safety.

You may also find it helpful to describe that as long as she realizes she's in danger, she will feel frightened, whether she has separated from the abuser or is living with him. If she's denying the danger, then these feelings aren't available to help her protect herself.

Rage

The woman who experiences profound rage and murderous thoughts of revenge against the abuser is in great pain. She feels helpless one moment and very powerful the next. She is capable of violence, and sometimes strikes out, while at other times she feels frozen, unable to act. She may feel guilt or shame for her desire to hurt the abuser. Frequently, what she desires is for the abuser to know how she has felt when she has been tortured, humiliated, battered and tormented.

When she shares her fantasies of revenge in the group meeting, nervous laughter often follows. It's valuable to acknowledge openly in the group that many women feel rage, and that talking about violent fantasies is not the same as acting them out, as the man who batters does.

For some women, coping with anger consumes most of their emotional energy. They can think and talk of little else besides the fury they feel toward the abuser. If they express concern about their emerging rage, you may want to confirm for them that uncontrolled anger can cause them serious problems. This is another opportunity in which you can emphasize your support for their safety, including the use of their anger to protect and care for themselves. You might say, "I'm worried about you, Gina. If you follow through with your plans to retaliate against him, it's you who will suffer the consequences. I hope you will choose to care for yourself instead."

You can also point out that prolonged anger can keep a

woman in a past relationship, preventing her from really experiencing the present or planning for the future.

Strategies for coping with anger and rage may become the "topic" for the evening. The suggestions offered by other group members are often the most useful and relevant to the woman who's struggling to control her anger. They may include journal writing, calling group members, physical exercise, visiting a relative or talking with a counselor. You may also want to suggest to the angry or enraged woman that she can begin to give herself some credit for the control she has already exercised and to build on those experiences of self-control.

"The Assistant"

One of the group leader's most knowledgeable, informal "assistants" is the woman who is "addicted" to the abuser, who has left and returned to him many times. She frequently appears to be cool, calm and collected. She speaks reasonably about the difficulties of leaving the abuser and is convincing in her advice to others to leave their abusive partners. Only after you turn the question of safety to her, and ask directly about her welfare, does it become clear to the group as a whole that this woman is still caught in the cycle of violence.

She knows all of the facts, yet she cannot stay out of the relationship. She is so detached from her feelings, especially those of compassion for herself, that she cannot apply the valuable advice she gives to others for her own benefit. Her self-esteem is in shreds; she is unable to mobilize her anxiety, anger or other feelings to help her to safety.

Occasionally, this woman can derive some strength from "teaching" others in the group. Seeing herself as an ally with the leader may help also to bolster her sense of strength and confidence. The drawbacks of this, however, can be her ability to hide behind her leadership role, becoming the helper who never gets help for herself. While you can give her recognition for the assistance she gives you and the group members, it's important to remain clear with yourself and with her that to remain solely in her "helper" role may only keep her stuck in the violent relationship. Encouraging and allowing her own needs to be expressed and accepted (i.e., allowing herself to feel confused, to feel danger, to feel sad, to feel frightened) is the first order of business for her in the group meetings.

Two Women's Stories

In this chapter, we have offered some suggestions for responding to the special needs of the group and its individual members. In conclusion we will share our experiences with two women who came to the group for a long time. In these brief descriptions you will recognize that one woman may have many special needs over a period of time.

Adele

When she first came to the group, Adele was in shock and was unable to speak or to look at anyone. She had been physically and emotionally abused with increasing severity during the past five years. Her life was in danger. Her husband had weapons with which to carry out his threats to kill her. Already he had nearly succeeded in choking her until she was unconscious.

Initially, Adele attended the group meetings weekly. It was a full year before she was able to speak spontaneously in a group meeting, although she did participate in structured exercises. During the second year she returned to the group on a sporadic basis, often taking the role of an informal co-leader. She spoke in a very quiet and timid manner, but what she talked about often concerned her deep fear and rage. During one meeting, after Adele had been attending the group for at least a year and a half, she cracked a joke! This was a remarkable, wonderful occasion, since she herself was aware of what she had done, and she realized that this was the first time she had been able to joke while talking about the abuser. Now, two and one-half years later, she sporadically returns to the group, especially when the abuser harasses her again by anonymous phone calls or by following her car. At these times she takes comfort in the companionship of other women who know the depth of her fear and who understand the exhaustion that comes from the constant battle with terror. And she offers to the group the inspiration of "making it through," despite the abuse and hardship. Others find they are given hope by knowing that Adele continues to feel better and that her life continues to have pleasure and meaning, despite the abuser's occasional attempts to disrupt it.

Sally

Sally came "straight off the road" to her first group meeting. She had been travelling for over 18 hours "without stopping for nothing but gas!" Only the day before she had been released from the hospital where she was recovering from injuries inflicted by her husband. Sally left her grown children, friends and high-paying employment behind in order to break the cycle of violence. She had reached the chilling realization that "the next time one of us was going to end up dead."

At first, Sally was experiencing severe depression and grief, including periods of losing hope and thinking of suicide. For several months she sat quietly in the meetings, occasionally crying when someone else's story reminded her of her daughter, her house, and of the friends she'd left behind. She was embarrassed to talk about her feelings of loss; she thought she was silly.

As she regained physical health, found work and made new friends through the group, Sally took great pleasure in playing "mother" to the younger members in the group, and she became an "assistant" to the leaders. She always gave out her phone number and was ready to go out on the town with those who were, like herself, lonely and frightened and struggling to put together a whole new life in a very strange environment.

"I don't think I could have made it without this group," she would tell us from time to time. For the six months in which Sally came to meetings weekly, the group provided a safe place in which she could share the pain of having to start all over, and the joys of making it through each day, feeling the new strength of self-esteem returning.

A year later Sally leaves us notes, or attends a meeting when her work schedule permits. Knowing that the group still meets in the same place at the same time each week is a valuable anchor for her. We remain a family that cares about her safety and well-being.

Notes

1. *The Diagnostic and Statistical Manual III* (Washington, D.C.: American Psychiatric Association, 1980), pp. 213–214.

Chapter 9

Topics and Brief Exercises

Topics

Because the women who participate in the group share the common experiences of physical and emotional abuse, they will also share questions and emotional responses that are similar in some important respects. The following discussion of topics often suggested by abused women is presented as a starting point to which you will add your creative and thoughtful perspectives. Each group will have its own unique style and "personality," and your response will be designed to meet the needs of the particular group you are with.

Can Counseling Help?

This is always a challenging topic, and one frequently raised. Since the group meeting *is* a form of counseling, you will be implicitly communicating that counseling can be helpful to many abused women by offering the group meetings. More controversial, however, are the questions concerning the effectiveness of counseling for the abuser and couples counseling.

Acquaint yourself with current theories and information about the effectiveness of various types of counseling and learn about the resources in your community.[1] Clarify your own values before introducing the topic to the group, and then be prepared to discuss honestly the information you have to offer. Most important, solicit experiences from the group members.

"My husband wants me to go to his counselor with him," a group member might say. "I don't know what to do." Ask if other participants have had experiences that might provide some information about this concern. Usually there will be a variety of responses, ranging from great optimism about couples counseling to strong reminders that the battering is not her problem to solve, and that he must get help for himself. You can offer information that groups for batterers do seem to have a positive impact on stopping the battering while the man is attending the group meetings. However, you will probably find that success stories of relationships continuing without further violence or threats of violence, with or without benefit of counseling, are seldom reported by group members (or in counseling literature). It is important to encourage women to put their own safety first in making decisions about counseling.

Do not deny or minimize the questions of danger and safety, particularly when discussing couples counseling. Sometimes, in an effort to be "fair," you may find yourself holding back relevant information. We recommend that couples separate until the abuser voluntarily seeks and participates in getting help to stop his violent behavior. Realistically, it may be a year or much longer before the abuser changes his pattern of violent behavior and learns to use anger management skills.

Alcoholism and Abuse

This is a huge topic which has only recently been studied and written about.[2] Nevertheless, you need to be prepared to consider at least some broad questions concerning the relationship between alcohol and abuse. Many women express the hope that "if he will only get sober, then he'll stop abusing me." Reports from group members suggest that this is a hazardous belief which often keeps women in danger. Many alcoholic men continue to batter after they stop drinking.[3] Some may stop battering once they stop drinking. However, until he stops drinking *and* battering, the man is dangerous.

If a group member initiates the topic of alcoholism, you can present some of the psychological defenses that are common to alcoholism and abuse. They are: denial, minimization, rationalization, and projection. Women in the group may recognize these defenses not only because their abusive partner relies on them, but also because they, too, may have begun to rely on them to cope with the abusive relationship.

The alcoholic woman who has been battered needs special reassurance that she is not at fault or to blame for the abuse she has experienced. She is likely to believe that her alcoholic behavior warrants punishment. She needs encouragement to care for her health and to seek the support and help of others who understand both alcoholism and battering.

Filling out Forms in the Group

Whether you choose to use any forms in your group that ask participants for information about themselves will depend upon funding requirements and your own interest in keeping statistics on your group. If the forms you use cause the group members distress, you may want to take time to give the issue full discussion in the group.

The discussion needs to be structured so that it doesn't deteriorate into a "gripe session" by a few that excludes other members. Instead, you can help to focus on issues stimulated by the experience of "being questioned," such as safety, confidentiality, intrusion, victimization or oppression. Leave room for the contribution of some women who have found that filling out the forms weekly helped them break through denial and become more honest with themselves about the severity of the abuse they've experienced.

Effects of Abuse on Children

Often a woman is reluctant to introduce her concerns about her children. She may be afraid that others will see her as abusive; she may consider herself a bad mother; or she may consider her worries irrelevant or unimportant.

As the leader, you will find it useful to introduce the topic of concerns about the children if several women in the group have children. Abused women need to know that their children will benefit by honesty about the violence they've witnessed or experienced, which includes speaking to children about "danger" and "safety," rather than "good" and "bad." Mothers need encouragement to protect the children from further exposure to violence in the home. The state laws and your policy regarding neglect and abuse of children can be discussed openly in the group. If you are clear and nondefensive about your role and the policies that you follow, then it is likely that the group members will hear and respond to your consistent emphasis on the rights of all members of the family to live in a safe and healthy environment.

Can Women and Men Really Like Each Other?

This question, and its partner—Are there any men out there who aren't abusive?—are often expressed as jokes. And, after the laughter has subsided, a clear, affirmative response is called for. Women who have been abused since childhood, and women

who have encountered many men who have abused them, come
to the group despairing that they will ever experience a nonabusive heterosexual relationship. Some women do not know
that there is an alternative to abuse.

If there is no one in the group who can recall or describe
some aspects of a "normal," i.e., nonabusive, relationship with a
man, then you can offer a perspective to the group.

For instance, you might say: "There are some men who
show concern and consideration of women's needs and feelings; who respect and appreciate women's strengths. There are
some men who have a willingness and ability to take responsibility for their feelings, including their anger. If you are not
focused on an abusive partner, you'll be free to identify a man
who is nonabusive."

Some women will be genuinely surprised to hear you state
that heterosexual couples do exist who share these values, both
in principle and fact.

The Progression of Violence

In most group meetings there is an opportunity to discuss
this topic. Your choice of focus will depend on what you have
planned and what the overall group composition and flow demands. If a woman (or several women) begins to talk about a recent escalation of violence in the relationship, including the use
or threatened use of weapons, she and others will benefit by a
discussion of the progression of violence. You may want to have
the group generate its own list or use one of the existing lists of
physical, sexual and emotional abuse as a starting point for
discussion.[4] The progression of violence is simply an ordering
of these lists from the least violent, i.e., shoving, slapping, criticizing, becoming jealous . . . to the most violent, i.e., imprisonment, choking, cutting with a knife, breaking a jaw. . . .

The critical information you will need to provide or reinforce in the discussion is that violence in a relationship usually
escalates over time. It rarely diminishes without intervention
and long-term help. You can also remind the group members
that when weapons are introduced by either person, the level of
violence is increased significantly. One of us has coined the
phrase "the lethality factor" to suggest the seriousness of this
escalation of violence. Death threats, acquiring weapons, or use
of weapons are clear danger signs that one or both of the partners in the relationship could be killed. Also, even if it is on the
low or mild end of the continuum of violence, a rapid escalation

of the level of violence is a warning sign not to be ignored.

Holidays and Anniversaries

It may be obvious to you, but it may not be to the women attending your group, that holiday or anniversary times are occasions for the emergence of strong feelings. In fact, you may find yourself feeling very awkward and hesitant when no one in the group wants to discuss upcoming holidays.

Persevere, at least long enough to ask the group members what plans they have for Chanukah or Christmas Eve; do they have plans for Thanksgiving Day? What special things might they plan for their birthday? How do they want to spend their first wedding anniversary away from the abusive partner?

For each major holiday, the group members can be helped to consider the choices available to them, beginning several weeks in advance. Some women will prefer to enjoy a holiday alone. "I'm looking forward to the first Christmas in fifteen years without his putdowns, and to doing things the way I want to this time." Only through the group discussion do other women begin to realize that they have been dreading the loneliness of a holiday "without him."

Often a discussion of loss, grief and mourning comes as a natural consequence to dealing with special "remembrance days," such as Father's Day or a child's birthday. You may be tempted to shy away from these painful feelings, hoping not to make her feel any worse than she already does. Have courage! Acknowledge how difficult it is to talk about such sad and angry feelings and encourage all of the group members to participate in the discussion. Such a group discussion may result in participants making plans to spend the holiday together, or for a few women to celebrate a birthday together.

Brief Exercises

The following brief exercises fall in a category somewhere between Topics and Exercises. They have a structure; the group leader takes an active role in guiding the group participants through the brief exercise; they elicit responses from all members of the group; they usually require about thirty minutes or less to complete.

You and your groups will generate your own list of brief exercises. These may be of help in getting started.

Creating a Pamphlet for Abused Women *

To get this exercise started, you can simply say: "If there were going to be a brochure or pamphlet on the table here (if your group sits around a table) that just exactly fits your needs, what would its title be? What kind of things would it say?"

Some examples of responses from our group meetings are the following:

- The Truth About Abuse
- Breaking Out of Isolation: Reaching Out to People
- Leaving the Abusive Relationship
- How to Protect Your Income and Property
- Don't Stay Alone
- Why People Are Violent
- The Physical Signs of Depression

As you can see, each of these suggested pamphlets is a topic in itself. The group members may choose to spend time exploring one issue in particular, or may enjoy sharing the experience of listing lots of "titles." It can be comforting to know that others have similar questions and uncertainties.

How to Tell When You're Afraid

This brief exercise can be used to help group members learn to identify their feelings. If they need help initially putting words to their feelings, you may want to say: "Some people notice that the muscles in their arms tighten when they are afraid. Or you may notice that it's difficult to concentrate. Can anyone else give an example of how she feels when she's afraid?"

Other women have reported headaches, memory loss, irritability, skin rashes and aimless wandering as some symptoms of their fear. The list can grow long.

In addition, this exercise may provide an opportunity to discuss emotional shock and the common symptoms associated with that condition, since a major contributing factor to the shock is fear. Or you can substitute other feeling words for the group to consider, such as sadness or anger.

The value of this brief exercise is primarily in the normalizing of emotions. The group members can learn that what they

---

* This exercise and "Keeping a Journal" on page 91 were created by Marianne Pettersen, who has been a co-leader of our group since 1983.

had thought was "crazy" might in fact be a normal, healthy, common response to danger, loss or injury.

Talking It Out

The focus of this brief exercise is to encourage women to reach out to others. The group leader initiates the exercise with a question: "When was the last time you talked with someone about the abuse you have experienced?"

After the group participants have had some time to think about this, you can ask for responses. Further encouraging words on your part might be: "Try to remember if you've talked with anyone this week about the abuse," or, "With whom did you last talk about the abuse?"

It is important to reinforce the efforts of women who've been abused to move out of their emotional isolation. However, keep in mind that it will not be good for a woman to hear uninformed or insensitive responses from people who do not understand her situation. It is not her job to educate others. Instead, she needs understanding, empathy and information. Encourage the group members to seek out and choose to talk with women from the group and others whom they have reason to believe will respond with at least some empathy for their experiences.

Keeping a Journal

This exercise has several parts. You can do a few or all of the parts depending on the time you have available and the specific needs of the group.

The leader begins by saying: "If you were to write in a personal diary or journal *one sentence* to describe how you were feeling or thinking, what would it say?

"What would it have said a year ago? Six months ago?

"What would the sentence be today?

"What might it say six months from now? A year from now?"

(You can change the times to be whatever seems appropriate to the group.)

There are frequently some women for whom this exercise seems to have special meaning. They respond immediately to the questions and benefit from having the chance to say outloud their private thoughts. Others find this exercise too abstract and have difficulty following the directions. The composition of the particular group meeting in which you try this out will determine how long you spend on it.

The following are examples of responses women in our group have made to writing journal entries for: a) one year ago, b) two months ago, c) today, and d) six months from now.

Linda:

a) I want out.
b) I could kill him.
c) I've got my kids and I'm not going back.
d) I'm doing well in school and things aren't as bad as I'd thought they'd be.

Barbara:

a) God give me strength.
b) I want to be left alone.
c) I wonder what it's going to be like.
d) I'm independent.

Mavis:

a) I'm losing touch with myself.
b) This can't go on forever.
c) I know I'm going to get out of this.
d) Gee whiz, I wasted a lot of time with that jerk!

Notes

1. See, for instance, Anne L. Ganley, *Court-Mandated Counseling for Men Who Batter: A Three-Day Workshop for Mental Health Professionals* (Washington, D.C.: Center for Women Policy Studies, 1981).

2. See Claudia Black, *It Will Never Happen to Me: Children of Alcoholics* (Denver: M.A.C., Printing and Publications Division, 1850 High Street, Denver, CO 80218, 1981).

3. Anne D. Shinkwin, Ph.D., in a study of Yupik Alaskan natives, found an exceptionally strong correlation between battering and alcohol. She concluded: "Although alcohol abuse alone does not account for the development of spouse abuse in Yupik society, it is the immediate precipitating cause for severe wife battering today. There is evidence that abusing couples who stop drinking also stop abusing." See "Homes in Disruption: Spouse Abuse in Yupik Eskimo Society," (Fairbanks: University of Alaska, August 1983), Report to Alaska State Senate. Manuscript on file at the University of Alaska, Anthropology Department, Fairbanks, AK 99701.

4. See Ginny NiCarthy, *Getting Free: A Handbook for Women in Abusive Relationships* (Seattle: Seal Press, 1982), pp. xxi–xxvi.

Chapter 10

Group Exercises

The following exercises are designed to respond to issues frequently raised by abused women who attend the group:

1) Cycle of Violence
2) Brainwashing
3) Valued Traits and Vulnerabilities
4) Saying No to Abuse and Saying Yes to Myself
5) Visualization—Staying and Leaving

The first three exercises are most useful with large groups in which there is little cohesion and in which the participants are at various stages of recognizing and understanding the violence they've experienced. The last two exercises each have special limitations and cautions connected with their use. As with the previous Topics and Brief Exercises, you will need to adapt these exercises to fit your personal style and the needs of the group you lead. It's important, however, that you understand and become comfortable with the concepts and goals of the exercises, so that you can communicate these clearly to the group participants.

Each exercise is presented with the same format:
- *Preparation and Limitations*
- *What the Exercise is About*
- *How the Exercise Helps*
- *Leading the Exercise*

Exercise One:

The Cycle of Violence

Preparation and Limitations

Time: This exercise may be completed in thirty minutes; however, the discussion generated by the subject may continue for another half hour or more.

Materials: You will need to use a blackboard or large newsprint and marker pen.

Limitations: Because this exercise presents information, it's tempting to lecture to the group. Resist this temptation whenever possible. Instead, elicit responses from the group members.

Of all the exercises, this one is the most adaptable to a variety of group sizes and needs.

What the Exercise is About

Many women express confusion about the recurring nature of the violence they experience in their relationship. It seems to them to be unpredictable and impulsive. "Living with him is like living with Dr. Jekyll and Mr. Hyde." They are similarly confused by the changes in their responses to their abusive partners. One day is a nightmare, the next is a "paradise."

The exercise describes three stages commonly experienced in battering relationships that follow one another and feed on each other, called the Cycle of Violence.[1] The stages are referred to as tension-building, violent actions, and honeymoon.

Denial, a powerful emotional defense, enables the stages to continue cyclically. Both partners use denial. The abuser avoids responsibility for his violent behavior by denying it has occurred. The abused woman tries to protect herself and the relationship by "forgetting" the violence. Often she denies the very real danger she lives with on a constant basis.

In the honeymoon stage of the cycle (if the couple still experiences this phase; for some it disappears after years of abuse), the denial is the strongest for both partners. It is understandably difficult for a woman to remember the violence she has experienced when her partner is contrite or charming. At other stages, it is often equally difficult for a woman to remember and not to deny that there have been honeymoon times of shared dreams and hopes and events.

How the Exercise Helps

This exercise allows the participants to identify and describe each phase of their relationships realistically. As each group member describes her situation, other members recognize similarities in the cycle and their isolation and shame diminish.

In addition, the exercise allows women to evaluate the current stage of a relationship for warning signs of a build-up toward violence, and to explore choices available to them based on this new information.

Leading the Exercise

Draw a circle on the blackboard or paper you've taped to the wall.

Divide the circle into three pie-shaped sections, explaining that the sections will vary in size based on each person's own experience.

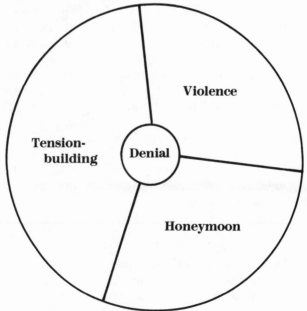

In the center draw a smaller circle which you will label "Denial." Then briefly explain the theory:

Leader: "In her book *The Battered Woman,* Lenore Walker summarized the experiences reported to her by many abused women. She found that there are certain fairly predictable stages in an abusive relationship. They are: the honeymoon, tension-building, and the eruption of violence. Perhaps some of you have experienced these stages. Let's talk about what each of these stages is like." (We reverse the order of these stages from Walker's discussion because most women can more readily identify the honeymoon stage than the tension-building stage.)

Some women may feel, at this point, that since they've left their abusive partner this exercise doesn't apply. Others may object that they're sure the violence is over and done with. It's important not to contradict the woman's perception of her situation. You might say:

✳ *Leader:* "I realize that your current situation doesn't seem to fit this picture. Perhaps you could think about whether you have ever noticed any of these patterns in your relationship."

Taking the lead again, you can begin to describe the honeymoon phase. You may want to include the following information:

Leader: "In the honeymoon period following an eruption of physical violence or extreme verbal abuse, the abuser may be sorry and apologetic. He says things like, 'I'm so sorry, honey. I only did it because I was drunk—or tired—or worked overtime. I promise you, it will never happen again. I love you so much, I just couldn't live without you.' He may cry, or offer flowers or candy. Or jewelry. Or he will reawaken old dreams by saying, 'We will take that trip.' 'We will move.' 'I will get a job.' 'I'll go to counseling.' "

Encourage group members to contribute their own experiences. Remember, some women may say that there is no longer a honeymoon phase: there is only tension and violence now. Research confirms that in some abusive relationships the honeymoon phase disappears.

When you feel that most women in the group have understood from their own or others' experiences the honeymoon stage, move on to tension-building.

Leader: "In the tension-building phase, which follows the honeymoon period, the abuser instigates minor incidents of physical or emotional violence that escalate. This stage may last anywhere from minutes, days or months to, occasionally, several years. At first you may deny what's happening, but at some point you begin to feel the tension, both within yourself and between you and your partner. In the beginning you may feel that you can control your partner's abusive behavior somewhat. By 'walking on eggshells' you may postpone his violent outbursts. But that fleeting sense of control disappears as the violence escalates.

"Still, you probably try to control the environment and other family members in an attempt to keep your partner happy and to slow the build-up of tension. You may try to keep the children quiet, prepare special meals or withhold 'upsetting' news from the day. You may make excuses for his behavior to yourself and to others, but these attempts don't help and may even backfire. For example, many women who've been abused will defend the abuser to their own friends and family. Feeling helpless, these valued supportive people often shy away from you. This then increases your isolation and makes you more dependent on the abusive relationship, but doesn't slow the buildup of tension as the batterer becomes increasingly frantic, jealous and brutal."

Ask group members to describe their experiences. Encourage group interaction.

Then, move on to your description of the times of violence.

Leader: "The final stage is the acute battering or abusive incidents. The batterer appears to be completely out of control. Many women, sensing this, react passively, trying to avoid further attack. Some women, however, fight back with widely varying results. Many women fear for their lives and often for the safety of their children and of other family members. This phase usually lasts from two to twenty-four hours but may continue occasionally for days or weeks."

Often, group members grow silent at this point, remembering the terror and helplessness of the abuse. You may want to elicit information about the duration of the violence stage, but it is not useful, at this point, to encourage lengthy individual accounts of violent episodes.

Be prepared to move on fairly quickly to a discussion of denial, referring to the inner circle on the diagram on the board (or paper).

Leader: "The middle, smaller circle is denial, which means pretending either that the abuse never happened or that it will never happen again. We put denial here, in the center of our diagram, to show how central denial is to continuing the cycle of violence. By coming to this group you're accepting that there is, or was, a serious problem in your relationship, so you've broken through your denial. The cycle will be weakened as long as you continue to remember that the abuse really did happen and really poses a serious threat to you. But whenever you find yourself thinking that the abuse never happened, or won't happen again within the relationship, then you're vulnerable to the cycle beginning all over again."

In concluding this exercise, if you have time, you may want to ask each group member to identify where she is *right now* in the cycle of violence. Sometimes it's helpful to stand by the diagram you've drawn and ask a group member to tell you when to stop as you move your finger slowly around the outer edge of the circle. For many women it is very surprising to discover that they can pinpoint with certainty the part of a stage they are experiencing; for example, "Right there! I'm on the line between honeymoon and tension."

Other women may feel more removed from the relationship, especially if they've been separated for some time. Emphasize that it often takes a very long time to be truly outside an abusive relationship and its cycle of violence. For example, a participant may realize that she is romanticizing an old abusive relationship by remembering only the good times. So she could be in the honeymoon phase even after a long separation. Another participant, long divorced, might be experiencing the tension-building phase as a result of renewed harassment by her ex-husband, or her fear of it.

Once again, encourage the group members to exchange information in order to provide an opportunity for each of the women to realize that she is not alone, nor are her feelings unusual or unimportant.

Exercise Two:

Brainwashing

Preparation and Limitations

Time: This exercise will require at least sixty minutes. Allow as much time as is possible in a group meeting without skipping a break.

Materials: You will need five to eight large sheets of newsprint, some felt pens, masking tape and a copy of the Chart of Coercion (see following pages).

Limitations: You may find it difficult to get through all of the items on the Chart of Coercion. As the group works on the first few, you may get a sense of those that will be most meaningful with this particular group composition. Focus on those that encourage the most interaction and response in your group.

Move the pace along and help the group members focus their examples on the topic being discussed.

What the Exercise is About

As a result of education by feminists about battering, therapists and the general public have a somewhat heightened understanding of, and concern about, the physical injuries inflicted on women in abusive relationships. Less attention has been given to the hidden injuries of emotional abuse, however. There are two reasons for the focus on physical battering: the immediate and serious danger of physical assault, including potential death; and the ease of recognizing physical symptoms, such as a black eye or a broken bone.

Most women who have left abusive relationships in which they were subjected to both physical and emotional abuse agree that the emotional abuse has the most debilitating long-term effects. However, for women who are still in abusive relationships, emotional abuse is difficult to recognize and name. Its unacceptable forms are hard to separate from the occasional and minor abuse present in most intimate relationships. The work of Diana E. H. Russell has helped us develop a framework in which to think about emotional abuse and to understand that such abuse of women by their intimate partners is remarkably similar to the torture and brainwashing of prisoners in war camps. In her book *Rape in Marriage*, Russell reprinted information from an Amnesty International publication, *Report on Torture*, indicating that brainwashing consists of a pattern of specific behavior.[2] Only now are investigators beginning to recognize that what was effective in prisoner-of-war camps is also effective in maintaining abusive relationships. Below is the Chart of Coercion that Russell reprinted.

Biderman's Chart of Coercion

General Method	Effects and Purposes
Isolation	Deprives victim of all social support [for the] ability to resist
	Develops an intense concern with self
	Makes victim dependent upon interrogator
Monopolization of Perception	Fixes attention upon immediate predicament; fosters introspection
	Eliminates stimuli competing with those controlled by captor
	Frustrates all actions not consistent with compliance
Induced Debility and Exhaustion	Weakens mental and physical ability to resist
Threats	Cultivates anxiety and despair
Occasional Indulgences	Provides positive motivation for compliance
Demonstrating "Omnipotence"	Suggests futility of resistance
Degradation	Makes cost of resistance appear more damaging to self esteem than capitulation
	Reduces prisoner to "animal level" concerns
Enforcing Trivial Demands	Develops habit of compliance

How the Exercise Helps

The exercise may help women recognize and identify emotional abuse. It may also help abused women understand that the impact and consequences of emotional abuse are great. Their reactions to such abuse can now be understood as normal responses to abnormal conditions.

In addition, the exercise will help abused women recognize exactly what is being done to them that causes their reactions, and recognize who is doing it.

Leading the Exercise

We each have different styles of leading this exercise, including the order of presentation. You will need to decide whether to introduce this exercise with the explanation of brainwashing first, or to give it later, after you have created your lists of examples from group members. We describe it here with the explanation following the group members' contributions.

In either case, you'll need large newsprint sheets on which you've written at the top of each one of the following categories of abuse, which we have slightly modified from the Chart of Coercion for easier comprehension:

- Isolation
- Focus on the batterer's potential anger
- Exhaustion, dependency, feelings of incompetence
- Threats
- Occasional indulgences
- Demonstration of "superiority" or power
- Degradation and humiliation
- Enforcement of trivial demands

Leave room under each heading to write the examples of the coercive behavior that group members have experienced with the men who batter them.

Pointing to "Isolation" as a heading on a sheet of newsprint you can say the following:

Leader: "We've talked about isolation in the group before—about the way many women who are abused are kept from seeing anyone except the man they're involved with. Perhaps tonight we can look more closely at exactly what that's like and how it's done. I'll explain, when we've completed the exercise, why I use these particular categories. I'd like each of you to give me some examples of how you were kept from being with other people or from telling them the truth, or even ways that you felt isolated. As you say them, I'll write them here on the newsprint."

Encourage women to say whatever comes to mind. Without making judgments or editing (except for space), write their responses on the newsprint so that all can see. If you have an active, verbal group, you may have to go on to the next category before all ideas are exhausted on this one. Take three or four minutes on each category. Just be sure each woman has the opportunity to have at least one of her ideas written on the sheet.

Pointing to "Focus on the batterer's potential anger" on the next sheet, you might say:

Leader: "Next I'd like you to think about the ways in which you have had to spend a lot of your time thinking about your partner, worrying about his reactions, and other ways that you focus your attention on him."

Again, encourage responses and write them as they are offered. Watch for women who are shy or soft-spoken, and help them express their experiences.

As you continue through the list, be prepared to add your own examples to help the group focus on the specific heading you're discussing.

Some examples given by abused women in our groups follow.

Isolation: He moved me away from my friends. He didn't want me to go anywhere unless he was with me. He would eavesdrop.

Focus on Him: I had to dress up for him. Give him sex whenever he wanted. I had to control the children so they wouldn't bother him.

Threats: He threatened to kill the cat. He said he'd have me committed. He said he'd burn down the house. He said he'd find me if I left. He threatened to leave me.

Occasional Indulgences: He allowed me sex only in the honeymoon phase. He allowed me to go to church on special occasions. He took me on a vacation. He bought me jewelry. Once in a while he really listened to me and seemed to care.

Degradation and Humiliation: He told me I'm too fat. He'd introduce me as his girlfriend, even though we're married. He'd call me names and touch me inappropriately in public. He put me down intellectually and sexually, and said I was ugly.

When all of the categories have been listed, explain the historical origin of the categories.

Leader: "After the Korean War, people were concerned

about why some American soldiers in prisoner-of-war camps were 'brainwashed' into believing certain ideas or propaganda. A team of people investigated the methods used to 'brainwash' the soldiers and found they used the same techniques that we have listed here. They were printed in a book about torture of prisoners and Diana Russell reprinted them in her book *Rape in Marriage*. We're not saying that your lives are the *same* as prisoners of war, or that you've been as thoroughly or systematically brainwashed as prisoners often are. But the techniques used are similar. They're pretty much the same ones used by any group or individual that wants to control or oppress any other group or individual. The problem is not just that the man loses his temper once in a while. What you have described here is much more than that. It's a regular campaign to control you, something like a reign of terror."

This is a lot of information for group members to absorb at once. Thread it into a discussion, or ask for comments every few sentences.

Women are usually impressed and sometimes shocked to learn of the similarities between the techniques of brainwashing and battering. They often ask whether the men who batter *know* they're carrying out their abuse in a systematic, successful way, and whether they plan it. The short answer to those questions is "I don't know," but you may want to turn the questions back to the women: "What do you think?" Some of the women will probably say the man has admitted to planning his actions, in order to intimidate or isolate them, for instance. But it doesn't really matter how consciously they plan. The result is his control and her feeling of helplessness and fear of leaving.

Depending on your time, you may want to discuss the effect that each type of "brainwashing" technique has on each woman. A variation on the exercise is to ask the group to fill in the same categories in reference to women as a whole, i.e., in what ways are women isolated from the mainstream of society and from each other? How are they encouraged to focus on pleasing men and protecting themselves from male anger and violence? Then discuss how women are thus prepared to intensify those same reactions when they're involved with a particular man.

A very important part of the exercise is a reminder that when women feel isolated, exhausted, threatened, etc., it's not because something is wrong with them, but because someone is doing something to them to cause them to feel that way. They need to say to themselves: "I'm exhausted, and that's not because there's something wrong with me. It's because this fear and tension are extremely wearing, and he's exhausting me. I'm afraid and feel degraded and helpless because he's threatening and humiliating and controlling me. Anyone would be worn out."

It's important to have a clear conclusion to this exercise. Recognizing that some participants may feel sad or angry as a result of their new level of awareness, you can now reframe the exercise to help each woman reexperience a sense of personal power and control over her own life.

Refer again to each heading or category on your adapted Chart of Coercion and elicit from the group members suggestions for counteracting the brainwashing technique. For example:

- *Isolation*: Telephone a friend. Enroll in a class.
- *Focus on batterer*: Listen to music I like.
- *Exhaustion*, etc.: Rest, read, eat regularly.
- *Threats*: Take self-defense class. Get a no-contact order.

Encourage group members to think of the small, everyday activities over which they do have some control. Remind them to consider what steps they can take to make their lives safer as well as more pleasurable.

Exercise Three:

Valued Traits and Vulnerabilities

Preparation and Limitations

Time: This exercise may be completed in thirty to forty minutes. It probably will not generate additional spontaneous discussion.

Materials: No special materials are needed for this exercise.

Limitations: The group leader may need to be quite active in assisting group members to contribute to this exercise, offering examples when necessary.

This exercise does not promote a great deal of group interaction, but rather encourages individual reflection in the safety of the group setting. You may find that the group members respond with thoughtful silences rather than active discussion.

What the Exercise is About

Researchers and clinicians are just beginning to study men who batter. Little scientific evidence is available now to explain, describe or predict their behavior. However, many women in groups have reported that one of the means used by their partners to control them is to undermine those strengths that first attracted their partners to them. If the woman uses these strengths or traits for her own or others' benefit, the abuser becomes jealous and will degrade, humiliate and attack her for doing so.

The abuser may systematically devalue those very traits that form the core of the woman's identity and her sense of strength and competence. For example, he may say repeatedly to the woman who has been supporting him, "You can't get along without me. You can't make it on your own. You are weak."

Similarly, a woman who has gained important recognition in her life for her intelligence may be called "stupid" and be humiliated in public when the abuser calls attention to gaps in her knowledge. Likewise, an industrious woman will be called lazy, a humorous woman called dull, and a compassionate woman called mean.

Some abusers belittle their partner's most important positive trait, turning it into a negative. Sexual attractiveness becomes "bait" or a "tease." Consideration is distorted as "goody two-shoes," and a nurturing woman is called a "push-over" or "weak."

This process of devaluation so thoroughly erodes the woman's sense of her self that eventually she can no longer offer the man that image which was initially attractive to him.

As a result of isolation in this abusive relationship, combined with fear and persistent criticism by the abuser, many women come to *believe* they are incapable of independent functioning. The resulting dependency on her part serves the abuser's need to control as well as to have "his woman to himself." But he loses the opportunity to lean on a strong woman, which may increase both his vulnerability and his rage.

How the Exercise Helps

This exercise assists women in recalling and reasserting the traits or strengths they most value in themselves. Group members can also experience a sense of positive self-worth and identify with the values presented by other participants. By recognizing that their valued traits are vulnerable to exploitation by the abusive partner, women can protect those strengths more adequately.

Leading the Exercise

The leader introduces the exercise directly, without discussing theory.

Leader: "I'd like you to take a minute or so to think of that one thing which you most value about yourself, that is, your strength or what you most like about yourself.

"I'm going to ask each person to say in *one word* that trait which you value most about yourself."

Pause for a minute or two, and add a few reminders such as "Just one word" to keep the group focused.

Leader: "Who would like to say what she came up with as that strength or personal characteristic that she values most about herself? We'll then hear from each person in turn."

Encourage the first volunteer by eye contact, perhaps someone who's been in the group before. Make your own contributions of your most valued trait, either at the end or when others are bogged down or shy. If members are having difficulty thinking of an admired quality, ask what they liked about themselves as teen-agers or young adults. Sometimes this is extremely helpful, and they remember a long-forgotten self confidence.

On your own piece of paper write each woman's name and her valued trait as it is given. Repeat the characteristic she names as you write it down, then move on rapidly. If a woman has difficulty, help her condense her phrase to one word. For example:

Participant: "I'm always doing nice things for people."

Leader: "You act in caring and thoughtful ways. Can you think of one word to describe that?"

Participant: "Yes, I'm caring."

Move quickly to hear what each woman has come up with. Then pause for a minute.

Leader: "Now I'd like to read back to you what you've told me about yourselves. Imagine that these words are describing one woman. That woman then is—" (Read the list: witty, intelligent, compassionate, gutsy, independent, caring, etc. There may be repeats of traits. It's fine to have the same or similar traits more than once.)

Leader: "That's quite a woman! Would you like to know that woman? Well, she's here. *You* are that woman. You are all those things—" (Read the list again.)

Notice that the word *you* refers here to both the individual *and* to the collective. The leader is reinforcing the individual woman's strength by combining it with those presented by the other women, thereby creating a "composite woman." It's a bit like borrowing strengths for a short time until one can regain or learn to have confidence in one's own strengths.

Some examples of the valued traits stated by group members are listed on the next page. Each list represents a single group in which the exercise was conducted.

Group 1	Group 2	Group 3
Studious	Creative	Determined
Independent	Determined	Strong sense of self
Outgoing	Mentally free	Have will power
Enduring	Spontaneous	Ambitious
Humorous	Strong	Humorous
Courageous	Mentally orderly	Friendly
Stylish	Free to be me	
	Sensitive	
	Enthusiastic	
	Have will power	

The second part of this exercise focuses on the vulnerabilities experienced by the women.

Leader: "Now I would like you to think a little about the ways in which this special aspect of yourself may also be your area of vulnerability. Are there ways in which that quality of loving or caring is used against you or exploited? Is your intelligence, humor or perseverance ever used against you in some way?" (Pause)

If no one volunteers a response, call on someone who seems fairly comfortable talking and begin a discussion with her. For example, "You have said that you like your industriousness. Can you think of any instance in which this trait has been criticized or exploited or used against you?" The woman may then become aware that she has been holding down two jobs, caring for the kids, keeping the home and so on. Even so, the abuser insists she is not industrious; he says that she is selfish, lazy, and that she spends too much time on others and not enough on him. She is being both exploited for the industrious person she is and constantly criticized for not being industrious enough, or for not centering her industriousness solely on him.

Each person who wants to talk may be encouraged to explore the question of her vulnerability. The group members will experience a commonality in having been exploited, just as they did in asserting their values.

To conclude the group exercise it's important to return to a strong assertion of the valued traits that the group members have stated earlier. To do this you might say:

Leader: "I'd like to remind you of what you told me at the beginning of the meeting. (Say the name of each member and her valued trait: Jane, you are intelligent; Mary, you are gutsy, etc.) This is quite a powerful, strong group of women."

This is usually a good way to end the group meeting.

Exercise Four:

Saying No to Abuse and Saying Yes to Myself

Preparation and Limitations

Time: This exercise may be completed in thirty to forty-five minutes.

Materials: None.

Limitations: It's important not to underestimate the powerful effects this exercise can have on group members. Use it only in a group meeting in which you are familiar with the participants and if you are confident in your ability to work with members who may feel out of control. The group will need your assistance to have a positive experience encountering their rage and their fear, the two emotions most strongly elicited by this exercise. Allow group members to find the level of emotional experience with which they are most comfortable. This exercise works best in a group with fewer than eight participants.

What the Exercise is About

To say "No" in a physically abusive relationship is to risk being injured by the abuser. Since the abuser often experiences his partner's "No-saying" as a loss of his control in the relationship, his response may be to reassert his power by the use of physical force and/or verbal abuse. The abuser frequently uses "crazy-making" statements such as "I know you don't really want to say No," or "If you say No, then I know you don't care about me." And sometimes the woman's attempt to say No triggers a marathon session of coercive behavior. Many abused women describe a state of profound confusion which has become so pervasive as to seem normal during the abusive relationship. As one woman explained: "I'm lying to myself if I say Yes. *He* thinks I'm lying if I say No."

How the Exercise Helps

The group provides a safe place in which a woman can experience saying No without risk of verbal or physical abuse or retaliation. In the group meeting she is offered an opportunity to move out of an isolated experience of *thinking* No into the supportive experience of *saying* No aloud with others.

This exercise also provides a chance to couple the experience of saying No with an affirmation of self, of saying Yes to one's self with others.

Leading the Exercise

It is important to remember how frightening it can be to an abused woman even to practice saying No. The experience may elicit responses of panic or rage that have been hidden for a long time.

You will need to pay close attention to each woman's experience of saying No. You can help her identify feelings, call on other group members for supportive feedback and guide the woman to a positive experience of self-determination. As the leader, you will set the tone for this exercise. You can intensify the experience of No-saying for a woman by encouraging her to try it again. Or you may move a woman out of a near-panic by supporting her courage to risk trying the exercise at all, and then moving on to others in the group.

The leader introduces the exercise directly, without discussing theory.

Leader: "For a little while we will practice saying No together. Each person will have a chance to try saying No just to see how it feels. I know this is not an easy exercise; however, I'd encourage each of you to give it a try.

"When you practice saying No, think of someone, something or a situation you wish to say No to. It can be anything. Then, just say it—say No and see what happens. Who would like to start?"

If no one volunteers, ask a member who's been to the group for at least several sessions if she's willing to start. Then work with each person in the group, encouraging everyone to take a turn. Each woman will simply say No and does not need to explain what she is saying No to.

After a woman practices saying No, ask her how she feels. Does she want to practice more? Does she feel okay about moving on to the next person?

Leader: "What was it like for you to say No? What feelings did it bring up?"

Occasionally a group member will experience a surge of anger as she says No. She may become fearful that she will lose control. Help her to put words to these fears so that she can experience one useful tool for gaining a sense of self-control. Assure her that she is in charge of her level of participation in this exercise.

Also, some group members report that they feel "shaky," that they are "trembling inside," or beginning to perspire. Discuss these physical experiences as normal signs of fear, reminding the group members that to say No to an abusive partner has often been dangerous and that they are remembering the fear they have felt in the past, even though they are now safe in the group meeting.

Encourage supportive feedback among members. For example, "You seemed to be more confident each time you said No. You looked like you really meant it!"

If anyone wants to practice more, encourage her to do so, time allowing.

To end this exercise it's very important to move into an affirmative mode. To do this you can suggest the following:

Leader: "Saying No to someone else can also be seen as saying Yes to myself. I'd like you to take a minute or two to think of something you might wish to affirm, or say Yes to, *for yourself*. I'll ask each of you to say Yes and add what it is you are saying yes to."

If the group needs an example, any of the following may be used: "Yes, I'm going to look for a job tomorrow." "Yes, I'm intelligent." "Yes, I am going to leave him."

As a grand finale to this exercise, a group cheer provides a corny but fun and powerful closing—everyone says Yes together. If the group has moved easily through the first parts of this exercise, and if no one is in crisis or great discomfort (e.g., crying, withdrawn), then this ending can be most effective.

Leader: "Before we close, let's all try saying Yes together, as a statement of our affirmation of ourselves. Okay, ready to say Yes? On the count of three—One, two, three—YES!"

Exercise Five:

Visualization—Staying and Leaving

Preparation and Limitations

Time: This exercise will require thirty minutes to complete. Additional time for discussion is also useful.

Materials: You will need to provide enough paper and pencils for the group members to have one of each. Having a blackboard or newsprint sheets helps, but they're not necessary.

Limitations: This exercise is best done in the first activity period of a session in order to provide sufficient time for additional discussion after the exercise. It is essential to give the group participants opportunity to express their reactions to the visualization.

If you have reason to believe that any participants might hallucinate, or have difficulty separating images from reality, do *not* use this exercise. In general, this exercise works best in small groups of women, most of whom are familiar with the group structure and who are not seriously disturbed (see Chapter 8) or in immediate crisis.

If you haven't conducted relaxation exercises in groups before, practice with friends until you're comfortable doing it. Also, have a friend give the instructions to you and notice your own reactions.

What the Exercise is About

One very critical issue for women in abusive relationships is that of whether or not to leave the relationship. Denial, fear, isolation, alternating hopefulness and helplessness, depression and economic problems may prevent women from actively making a decision about leaving.

Women often feel overwhelmed by indecision, which adds to their feelings of powerlessness. Women who've been in abusive relationships may not believe in their ability to make sound, autonomous decisions—or stick to them.

Even after a decision has been made, women who've been abused tend to blame themselves for not making a different decision or for not acting more quickly. For example, women who have left for good often berate themselves for having stayed so long, instead of focusing on the courageous action they've taken. Or they may worry constantly about the possibility that they'll weaken and return. Although this is not an unrealistic fear for many, allowing it to dominate their thinking may actually enhance the possibility of returning. Constant worry and self-interrogation contribute to the enormous physical and emotional tension experienced by women who've been abused. And they often know very few, if any, healthy ways of reducing their physical and emotional tension.

How the Exercise Helps

In the supportive atmosphere of the group, each participant is given the opportunity to consider leaving the battering relationship or to discuss her desire to stay. Also, she may review and accept previous decisions. Since each person's imagery will be unique, participants can be in any stage of the decision process about whether or not to leave an abusive relationship.

The exercise teaches and provides an experience of relaxation and reduction of muscle tension.

Leading the Exercise

Throughout the exercise, use words that provide choices for the group members as you give the instructions for relaxation and imagery, e.g., "if you like," "you might want to," "you could."

Also, remember to give permission to participants to leave their eyes open if they prefer.

As you begin to pass out paper and pencils to each woman, give the following instructions:

Leader: "I'm going to ask each of you to write things which are for you to read later on. You will not need to share this with anyone, unless you want to. Please draw a line vertically down the middle of the paper." (Demonstrate this.) "The first column you can label 'staying' and the second column 'leaving.' " (Demonstrate on blackboard or on paper.) "Does anyone need help?

"It is fine to write in your own language, if English is a second language for you. And spell so *you* can read it, not for someone else. This is for you.

"Now I'd like you to write at least one reason in each column. In the first column list some of the reasons you have or had for staying in the relationship." (Pause.) "In the second column write some of the reasons you might have, or have had, for

leaving the relationship. It's important to write at least one reason in each column. Write more than that if you can."

(Allow about five minutes for this, but proceed more quickly
if all are finished writing.)

Leader: "I'd like you to put the paper aside now and to clear
away your purses or other things around you. You can shift
your chairs and your bodies however you like, to make yourselves more comfortable. Many people are most comfortable
with both feet flat on the floor and with their hands resting on
their lap. Feel free to shift at any point to make yourself more
physically comfortable."

Each series of dots [. . . .] in the following instructions
indicate pauses to take as you lead the exercise.

Leader: "It's most relaxing to close your eyes, if you're
comfortable doing that. Otherwise, pick a spot on a wall and concentrate on that spot. If you have contact lenses, you'll probably
want to open your eyes from time to time or to remove your
contacts.

"Now, just begin to pay attention to your breathing. Follow
your breath through your whole body. Imagine that you are
breathing *in* relaxation, which passes slowly through your
whole body. Then breathe tension *out*, through your toes. You
can slow your breathing some, if you want to relax further."

Your voice will slow down and drop in volume as you relax,
so you could ask the participants to raise their hands any time
they can't hear you. Since they are better able to concentrate
now and will probably hear you well anyway, you can allow your
voice to soften naturally as you go. . . .

Continue when most participants seem comfortable and
more relaxed.

Leader: "As you follow your breathing, you might notice a
spot in your body where you are holding tension, or that feels
tight or painful or uncomfortable. Concentrate on one of those
areas and imagine warming that area and melting that tension.
Just enjoy the relaxing feelings that you are creating for yourself. . . ."

Leader: "And now, if you want to, picture an object or scene
that is calming or relaxing for you. . . . Just enjoy the feelings of
relaxation you are creating for yourself. You can return to these
feelings at any point in your day-to-day life. . . . by simply taking
a deep breath and then thinking of this object or scene. . . . You
can also return to this object or scene at any point in this exercise, if you begin to get tense, or if you don't want to go on with

any of the suggestions I may make. . . ."

Leader: "If you want to, picture the abusive relationship you've experienced. . . . Imagine your life with that partner. . . . Picture your life as specifically as possible. . . . See the good times. . . . Now picture the bad times and the abuse. . . . Imagine your relationship with any children you have (or might like to have). . . . Notice your relationships with friends. . . . With any co-workers you may have. . . . You might want to go through one entire day and picture in detail what that day is like. . . . In the morning. . . . In the daytime. . . . At mealtime. . . . In the evening. . . . At bedtime." (Longer pause.)

Leader: "Now imagine instead that you decide to leave this relationship. . . . Picture your life as specifically as possible. . . . See the good times. . . . Time alone. . . . With friends. . . . Doing the things you never had time for or were afraid would seem silly. . . . And also notice the sad or lonely times. . . . Imagine your relationship with any children you have or would like to have. . . . Notice your relationships with co-workers. . . . with neighbors or relatives. . . . the possibility of finding a new loving relationship. . . .

"Now it is time to return *very* slowly and at your own pace to this room. . . . You might want to wiggle your toes and fingers. . . . And when you're ready, open your eyes and look slowly around the room."

Pause until everyone has opened her eyes.

Before discussing this experience, ask participants to use what they learned from this exercise by adding one or more reasons to both columns on their list of reasons for staying and leaving. Wait for them to write.

Ask for a volunteer to discuss her reactions to the exercise. Then ask the person next to her, and continue until all who are willing have spoken. Some questions to elicit discussion are:

Leader: "What was the most surprising (or painful, or exciting) image you had?

"Do you feel more relaxed now than when we began?"

Reassure anyone who doesn't that some people get tense with this kind of relaxation technique, and they can instead reduce body tension through vigorous exercise. Others may find that doing very brief relaxation exercises on a daily basis may enable them to reduce tension after a time.

You might begin a discussion of participants' reactions to the exercise by asking: "Can you imagine doing this relaxation on your own, whether with or without the future imagery?"

"Can you imagine doing this relaxation on your own, whether with or without the future imagery?"

"Were you able to add reasons for staying or leaving to your original lists?"

As noted in the introductory remarks to the exercise of Valued Traits and Vulnerabilities, exercises that encourage reflection and foster a sense of personal awareness and discovery may not generate lively group discussion or interaction. You will need to be prepared to move on in the meeting to consider additional topics or concerns introduced by the group members.

Notes

1. Lenore E. Walker, *The Battered Woman* (New York: Harper & Row, 1979), pp. 55–70.

2. Diana H. Russell, *Rape in Marriage* (New York: Macmillan Pub. Co., 1982), p. 184. This material was reprinted from Amnesty International, *Report on Torture* (London: Gerald Duckworth, 1973), p. 49.

Part Four

Continuing Challenges

Chapter 11

Groups for Specific Populations

This book has assumed that your group is composed of women who differ in age, race, lifestyle, religion, values and capacities. Most communities won't have the luxury of providing groups for specific populations of women who have been battered, but where that is a choice, we hope you'll consider making a special effort to form groups of whatever type are most needed in your community. Where such groups are not feasible, you may be able to incorporate information and ideas from this chapter into your mixed population group.

Our discussion is brief because our experience and knowledge about each population are limited. We have chosen to include this chapter in the book, even with quite incomplete information, because of our belief in the importance of sharing insights and experiences as they develop. We hope some of you will be encouraged to begin such groups and learn as you go along, and that others will be inspired to write about the expertise you may already have about work with homogeneous groups, so we may all learn from each other.

As you read through this section, notice the liberal use of "may," "most," and such words as "tendency." There are certain customs and traits that are more or less common within certain homogeneous groups. That's quite different from saying, "This is the way *'they' are*," and that you can predict, therefore, certain behavior or responses or problems. Our comments and suggestions are designed to increase your sensitivity to individuals, and in some cases that will be reflected by your special effort to offer groups for individuals who are similar in certain respects.

Groups for Women of Color

If you live in a community with a multiethnic population you may be instrumental in starting a group specifically designed for Latina, Asian, Black or Native American women, or an even more narrowly defined population, such as Vietnamese or Chicana. Women of color have benefited from mixed-race groups, just as white women have. In some instances the face-to-face experience with women of all colors and ethnic backgrounds has been the most effective way of emphasizing that battering knows no barriers of culture, lifestyle or race. Yet, there are some disadvantages of the mixed group.

Special Issues

Black, Asian, Latina and Native American women may be acutely aware of the discriminatory way that men of color are treated by the justice system, so their reluctance to report or to urge action by prosecutors may have a different meaning than a similar hesitation by white women. In a racially unified group, women may feel comfortable speaking frankly about such misgivings, whereas in a mixed group they may be silent on the subject.

Some minority racial groups have more extended family networks than the majority of white ethnic groups. Such networks may be both an advantage and a disadvantage for women who have been abused. For a woman who wants to leave an abusive man, a large, close-knit family might provide the advantage of warmly welcoming her for an extended visit. Such support in a safe environment may make the essential difference in a woman's ability to think clearly about her choices. On the other hand, if the family members are unified in discouraging a woman from leaving her partner, making a break from the abuse might mean leaving her entire family, as well.

A woman of color may feel comfortable only in certain neighborhoods, restaurants, taverns or churches where people of her community—including the man who battered her—congregate. It will be particularly hard to stay away from places the violent man frequents and from people who will tell her about his loneliness or his new woman. She may, therefore, be more at risk of being threatened by him or of being wooed back into the relationship.

In any case, some women of color feel more free to discuss these questions in a group of women whose common culture enables them to understand their situation, rather than in a mixed group.

Topics

There are many special issues that a group for women of color can explore, in addition to those mentioned previously. For instance, women of color are discriminated against both as women and as members of their racial group, so they come into a relationship with a history of institutional abuse by society. The group may want to discuss the significance of those experiences in relation to battering.

In this group you may want to modify some of the exercises or topics to clarify the differences and similarities between the various kinds of institutional abuse and individual abuse. For instance, you may want to modify the "brainwashing" exercise to fill in each category with examples of how each woman experiences isolation, threats, etc., as a woman, as a person of color, and then, how each has been subjected to brainwashing by a partner. Some women are able to forgive themselves for having stayed in abusive relationships by understanding how institutionalized abuse of women and people of color may have contributed to their special vulnerability to individual abuse.

This kind of discussion or exercise can lead to feelings of hopelessness or bitterness, neither of which will be useful to maintain over the long haul. To counteract that effect, set aside time during the last half hour of the group meeting for participants to discuss ways that such brainwashing and oppression have been overcome by women of their race. The group leader should do a little homework, if necessary, to discover good models in past and contemporary lives of women of color who overcame seemingly overwhelming obstacles in their lives.* Consider, also, recruiting formerly battered women to talk to group members about their experience of changing their lives.

A woman of color may be acutely aware of the pain inflicted by white people and institutions on men of her race, and feel responsible for compensating for it. In addition, the woman may feel guilt if she's able to find work and her man isn't. This might be so, even if the man hasn't looked for work, and even if the woman herself is underemployed and underpaid.

Some women may feel that they have no choice about staying with the abusive partner, because divorce is out of the question in their community, or that battering is inevitable because

* This idea was contributed by Addei Fuller.

"That's just the way Black/Hispanic/Native American/Asian men are." A group may reinforce those beliefs when they're expressed by a woman who feels helpless, and participants and leaders may become discouraged. The leader can help the other women remember that there are women in every racial and ethnic group who have separated from violent spouses, just as there are men who don't batter. In addition, some community leaders in every racial group understand the necessity for leaving a man who batters. If you can't find such models within the local ethnic community, look for national figures or leaders in the nearest large urban area.

When it is a necessity to make the frightening decision to either risk one's safety by staying with a violent man or to give up the security of one's community, that situation can be squarely faced with the help of women who are thoroughly familiar with resources and alternatives. Group leaders can help a woman recognize both the possibility and necessity of that choice, and may be able to help her find another place to resettle, or arrange temporary shelter and locate organizations of women of her racial group to ease the transition. The resettlement might be in a different city or in a new neighborhood within the same large city.

Leadership

If you are a woman of color who has knowledge about battering and group leadership experience, your sensitivity to other women of color will enable you to make appropriate modifications of the ideas in this book. If you're white and you're part of a shelter or other service agency, we hope you'll already have made a special effort to develop a racially mixed group of co-workers, one of whom might become the leader of this special group for women of color. If not, you will need to search for a leader within the appropriate community. We assume that if you've felt the need for this particular group, you'll already have been in touch with appropriate community clubs, social organizations, churches and agencies.

If you're unable to pay leaders and childcare workers, it may be difficult to find women willing to provide the services on a volunteer basis. You may be able to recruit women of color who have attended mixed groups, or who have been in shelters, to learn on the job how to lead a group. Even though they may not have leadership training, they can bring sensitivity to many important issues because of their own experience of being abused and their awareness of issues related to women of color.

Ideally, each group would be co-led by two women of color, but if the only potential leader is a woman of color whose inexperience makes her reluctant to take on the role, you'll have to compromise. A white woman with knowledge of battering and group work can help in any of these ways: provide a course of training for the woman of color; become a temporary co-leader with her until she feels secure or a co-leader emerges from the group; or act as consultant to her.

As an example of our own experience, one of the (white) authors co-led a group for Black women with a Black woman who had little group experience. After eight weeks of working together, the white woman dropped out, as planned, and was replaced as co-leader by a Black woman who had no previous group therapy experience, but who had been a participant in a mixed group for battered women.

It's also important for the childcare workers to be people of color. If there is only money to pay one or two people, perhaps it should go to the childcare person. It's usually more difficult to find people who view childcare as intrinsically rewarding than to find volunteer leaders, since leaders may feel there's something in it for them, even without pay. Deciding how minimal funds should be distributed can be difficult. A review of Chapter 5 on organizing childcare may help resolve some problems.

Groups for Women of Faith

Whether or not women in your group attend religious services or consider themselves members of religious congregations, spiritual issues are likely to be prevalent because of childhood or adult religious training. In a mixed group they may be expressed or not, depending upon how safe it feels to do so. A group leader should be open to expression of spiritual concerns and encourage women to respect each others' beliefs, whether or not they agree. But a group specifically designed for women of certain religious backgrounds can guarantee a high degree of safety in discussing them. Such a group should be run by a clergywoman or laywoman who is familiar with the appropriate religious doctrines of the members and who has been trained to work with women who are abused. Since no one can be an expert on all religions, this might mean limiting the group to Christians, Moslems, Jews or some other relatively homogeneous religious group. The leader's familiarity with various interpretations of the pertinent scriptures may open up new possibilities for the participants.

A woman who has accepted religious interpretations from a minister, rabbi or priest (or a husband) who has an interest in keeping her "in her place" may be surprised to learn some of the contradictory messages that are in the scriptural texts. Just knowing that other people with a strong faith and religious background also believe in a woman's right to be safe may start a woman moving in a different and more positive direction.

It is not useful to argue with a person who holds strongly to a particular belief and doesn't seem open to new information. Unless you are an expert, you should be careful not to be drawn into competition over quoting scriptural texts to prove a point. Prior to beginning a group for women of faith (or any group) try to find clergy people of various denominations who are opposed to woman battering and who will encourage women to create safety for themselves and their children. When appropriate, refer group members to them, so they'll have another experience with a religious authority who believes in their right to be safe.

Any of the exercises and topics in this book might be useful for women of faith, but the group leader will probably also add topics that are pertinent to the religion of her group members. Some examples are justice; forgiveness; obedience to scriptural commandments, clergy and husbands; scriptural interpretations of husbands' respect for wives; restrictions on separation and divorce.

Groups for Disabled Women

Disabled women may find it impossible to get to a group even if you have provided a facility with a wheelchair ramp, someone to help a blind woman in and out of the building, and an interpreter for the deaf. Additional restrictions in transportation and isolation may still prevent their getting to the group. The problems of mobility and independence are huge, and few communities have begun to try to overcome them. When resources are slim, it is tempting to postpone reaching out to people with special needs who may require us to do extra work and learning. But if volunteers or grant money can be found to put extra effort into outreach, the rewards may be great. At the least, we suggest that you be in touch with organizations that are designed to give assistance to physically disabled women in order to find out what their needs are. If you organize a mutual-help group, try to recruit at least one leader from the disabled community.

It may be that organizing work can be done in settings where physically or developmentally disabled people are gathered together for rehabilitation or in semi-independent living groups. So far, we haven't heard of any group that has done so, but the need is surely there, and you may be the first to take up that challenge.

One of us has assisted women in the deaf community in organizing a Safe Homes system. We hope there will be a group for deaf women, in time. The problems are great and the community is closed and small, presenting problems similar to those typical of small racial communities and many rural areas. Everyone seems to know everyone else and their business. In addition, isolation from most hearing people, the lack of educational opportunities and developed reading skills among some deaf people, and relative lack of access to television and radio have meant that many deaf people have not absorbed the important social changes of the 1960s and '70s. This is especially true for women who stay at home. The result is a politically and socially conservative community which may, more than others, resist the idea that women can make their own decisions and live independently, insisting on their right to be treated with respect.

If you're part of an organization that serves hearing women who are abused, we strongly urge you to investigate purchase of a TTD (Teletype Device for the Deaf) so that deaf women can call you for information and referrals. Use of a TTD requires less training than a typewriter, and you can get information about its use from local or nearby organizations for the deaf.

When working with a population that has special difficulties of mobility, communication, economics or belief systems, begin slowly and listen closely. As you discuss the potential for change, either with other organizers or with individuals who have been victimized, you may feel at first that you're in the midst of a huge "yes-but" game. Each suggestion may be met with another seemingly insurmountable problem. Let yourself experience the sense of helplessness, frustration or anger coming from the group you're working with until you're sure you understand most of the special difficulties. Then be sure they know that you understand.

Once they realize you're not underestimating how difficult their situations are, they'll be ready to join you in brainstorming how to meet the group's special needs. Many problems will not be immediately resolvable, but you can remind the group that important social change has often begun when individuals stubbornly broke through their despair and the assumptions that nothing could or should be done.

Groups for Teen-Agers

Only recently has public attention been directed to the problem of teen-aged women being battered by husbands and boyfriends.[1] Perhaps the problem has not been taken seriously because teen-aged women are rarely taken seriously by adults, and their relationships are viewed as transitional and unimportant. Some adults may view teen-aged women as free to exercise many options since they have "the rest of their lives" to explore job opportunities and relationships. The young women themselves often have a different perspective. They may feel boxed in by parents, school pressures, lack of job skills and the men in their lives.

Teen-aged women have concerns similar to those of adult women, and often such concerns are even more pressing for teens. In addition to the limitations placed on their freedom by the abusive men in their lives, they are especially likely to be underemployed, underpaid and lacking in marketable skills and education. The immediate options for many of them are generally more limited than those of many older women. Like adult women, they're reluctant to admit to the violence in their relationships. If they do acknowledge the violence, a parent or other adult authority may forbid the relationship to continue.

All women have been exposed to the powerful idea that finding and keeping the one true love of their lives is central to the good life. Adult experience and education temper many women's faith in the idea, but for teen-agers it is often still an unyielding belief.

All women have also absorbed, to varying degrees, the idea that a good woman is a "pure" woman, i.e., not sexual, or at the very most sexual with only one man. As we grow older many of us change those ideas, but for many teen-aged women, it is a potent group norm. In some ways, a woman in her teens is subjected to the same group pressure as is experienced by an adult in a small, homogeneous community. "Everyone" is likely to know she's having sex with a boyfriend; "everyone" will know if they break up, and will know and disapprove if she begins to see a second boyfriend and has sex with him. She may be called a "slut" by former friends or she may take that label on herself, having internalized the norms of the group. If a young woman believes she must choose among a bad reputation, a violent boyfriend or no boyfriend at all, she may prefer to face a continuing violent relationship to the other alternatives.

An additional problem for adolescents is that many shelters are reluctant to house them because the staff fears legal complications. Services are even less available to them than to adult women who are battered.

Allowing for the fact that many young women drop out of school, especially if they're married or pregnant, schools are still the one place where the largest number of young women (and men) can be found in one place. Many schools have steered away from classes on interpersonal issues, but others are opening up to the topics of incest, rape, romance and marriage. If you want to reach teen-agers, your organization might consider working with school staff to develop a class or a series of group meetings within schools. You might have the most success in approaching alternative schools. If you approach traditional public schools, try counselors or classes in home economics, social studies, health, psychology, sociology, sex education or current events. In some communities, traditional organizations for young women are changing and you may interest Girls Clubs, Girl Scouts or other organizations for teen-aged women in setting up classes or groups which you could conduct or to which you might act as a consultant.

One of us co-led a group on "Addictive Love and Abuse"[2] for young women in a teen-aged pregnancy program at an alternative school. The young women were recruited by word of mouth and by school counselors who had knowledge that the young women had been abused. Participants were apparently drawn to the group by the phrase "Addictive Love," and the prospect of being with friends.

Groups for teen-agers require a high degree of flexibility in both substance and structure. In a public school class that draws from the general population, a class structure will probably seem less invasive of family privacy and therefore less threatening to staff and parents than a group structure. Trust and confidentiality are important issues in schools, since the students may know each other and fear exposure of private matters they discuss in the group. Encourage them to trust their own judgment about discussing personal issues.

Although this work is difficult, we feel strongly that it is im-

portant. If the next generation is to create families that are more
caring and safe than those we have now, it is essential to work
with young people and to bring information about battering
into the schools at all age levels.

Groups for Recovering Alcoholic Women

Although none of us has led a group using an AA format, we
know of one group for women who are, or have been, abused and
who are also recovering alcoholics. We describe it here because
of the great potential for more such groups. The group was started by an active member of Alcoholics Anonymous.* She asked
a few friends in AA to join her in her home to talk about the
violence they had experienced in relationships. It began with
three women, and the numbers steadily increased each week
until there were twenty-five women at the fourteenth week's
meeting. Most women attended regularly, and most of them are
members of AA.

This group for battered women is the only one we know of
that has increased its numbers dramatically from the start and
has had a large number of participants who continue to come
each week. That degree of response has been achieved with no
formal advertising, no funds and no sponsoring organizations.
Although one participant provided leadership for the first few
meetings, the group, like others composed of AA members, uses
a self-help model in which all participants take responsibility
for the conduct of the meetings.

The facilitator makes it clear that everyone is welcome to
participate and express feelings and that she takes responsibility for preventing inappropriate problem-solving or monopoli-
zation by one or a few people. Unlike AA meetings, there is some
confrontation and interaction among members, although support continues to be a major purpose.

The woman who hosts the meeting asks someone to facilitate each week. Whoever is facilitator for a particular meeting
opens it with introductions; the host then reads a page from the
book *Everyday A New Beginning*, and asks a participant to read
from the lists of abusive behavior in the introduction to *Getting
Free*.[3] (The order of these lists is changed, beginning with the
least threatening, emotional abuse, then physical abuse, and
finally the most threatening, sexual abuse.) The reader may or

---

* Bernadette Willman began this group and provided the description of it.

may not comment. The facilitator then asks whether particular women have things they want to talk about, or she may ask for topics. Some topics that have been discussed are pain and progress, anger, sexual abuse, hurt, "enabling" the batterer, describing the abuse (a device to break through denial), trust and characteristics of abuse.

The facilitator encourages women to exchange telephone numbers and talk to each other during the week, and she explains that participants may experience emotional swings ranging from feeling "high" to panic, as a result of the meetings.

Coffee and cookies are available throughout the meeting. Some women go in and out throughout the two hours; and there is no formal childcare, so children may be heard off in a bedroom. Some women arrive early and many stay for an hour or more after the formal meeting has adjourned with a recitation of the serenity prayer. To the uninitiated or to professionals who are accustomed to the kind of structure we have advised in this book, this might seem chaotic, but it works well for this group. When a few group members discussed the group format with one of us, all agreed that several aspects of the group are likely to work well only within an AA context.

This group seems to work particularly well because AA women have learned not to be afraid of groups and have made meetings a priority. They welcome the use of a certain amount of ritual, as well as the free flow of ideas, mutual nurturing and the understanding of women who are experiencing pain similar to their own. Participants are accustomed to speaking briefly, and about their own experiences, as well as encouraging each other, so facilitation is relatively easy.

Many feminists may react negatively to the AA idea that alcoholics admit to being powerless over alcohol and that their lives have become unmanageable (Step One of the Twelve Steps). If this idea is carried over to battering it could seem to disempower women who are battered. However, we believe it is properly interpreted as a determination to make life manageable and a recognition that a woman who is being battered is powerless to stop the battering and may be powerless to leave the man who won't stop it, *without the help of someone else.* That someone else may be a "higher power"—and "higher power" may be interpreted as a group, an idea of liberation, dignity, or God, or some other value or vision. Recognizing she needs help is the first step toward safety for many women. We hope many other women in AA will form groups to free themselves from abusive men.

Groups for Lesbians

Battering between lesbians has, until quite recently, remained largely unacknowledged.[4] Some lesbians have used services for battered women without revealing their sexual orientation because they're wary of the kind of reception they will receive if they say that they're lesbians. They may also be reluctant to admit that lesbians can be violent to each other. The fear of a negative reception is valid, since counselors or other battered women may be as homophobic (fearful of gays and lesbians) as anyone in a homophobic society. The National Coalition Against Domestic Violence, as well as some state organizations and individual shelters, are currently dedicated to eliminating homophobia within the battered women's movement, so that shelters can be safe for all women.

Special Needs for Confidentiality

In the early years of the battered women's movement, it was comforting to believe that women would not be violent to each other. Or perhaps those who were violent could be dismissed as "other"—not representative of lesbians. However, what little-information is available indicates that battering is a serious problem among lesbians (and gay men). We know battering isn't a problem just for the "others," but occurs, as heterosexual battering does, in all classes and lifestyles.

Confidentiality is an especially important issue for lesbians. In addition to all the concerns that heterosexual women have, many lesbians must also guard the secrecy of their sexual orientation, since exposure might result in the loss of a job or the threat of a child custody battle. And public awareness of private relationships is a particular danger in a community where everyone seems to know everyone else. In many locations lesbians are part of a very small community, and there may be only one public gathering place in which it's possible to feel free about dancing, talking or being with other lesbians.

In such a situation, breaking off a relationship may result in a special desire to protect the violent partner's reputation. Friends may expect an explanation for the break-up, and refusal to acknowledge the battering may place the abused woman in a dishonest or alienated position in relation to friends of hers or of the couple. Or the abused woman may want to talk to friends about ending the relationship, but she may have no friends except those shared with her violent partner, who may threaten her with more battering if she tells.

In addition, after the break is made, there may be few people the abused woman can spend time with. There may also be few places she enjoys going where she won't encounter the former partner, nostalgic reminders of her or, at the very least, conversations about her. (This hazard may even include the drop-in battered women's group, where there is no screening process, if the partner chooses to attend.)

Lesbians who are battered, in contrast to heterosexual women, may not be able to assume safety even in a group for lesbians who are battered. A female partner may *feel* she's the abused one even if she's the abuser. She may appear at a group her lover has sought for sanctuary and not identify herself as an abusive person nor as the partner of the victim. The partner who is abused, on the other hand, may be too intimidated to disclose the relationship or the battering.

This potential situation poses a distinctly sensitive issue for the group leaders. Ideally, each community would have a group for lesbians who batter and more than one group for lesbians who are battered. Women who clearly identify themselves as abusers would be referred to the appropriate group and excluded from the others. Where each woman sees herself as victim and not abuser, each could go to a separate group for women who are battered.

This plan would be difficult to put into action, using the model we have described, because our model supposes a drop-in group with no prior screening. It may be that groups for lesbians—even drop-in groups—should require screening. This brings up numerous problems beyond the scope of this book. (There have been some groups composed of both lesbians who are abused and who are abusers—but not couples, as far as we know—and it may be that this model will develop as the most useful format for women.)

Assuming you have only one group, that it is for lesbians who are abused, and that you haven't set up a screening process, you'll need to be sensitive to the possibility of couples appearing separately or together. A policy of only one party to a couple in the group and first come, first served, may help. You may have to ask, "Are there any couples here?" and then explain, "This is not a couples group, and since we can't accommodate couples we'd like (the second to arrive) to leave and talk to us later about a referral to private counseling." If the couple has come together, ask them to decide which of the two should stay in the group.

Other Problems

A woman's first sexual relationship with another woman may present pressures to stay together. If she is unwilling to come out of the closet to anyone but her partner, the thought of breaking up the relationship may be especially stressful. She may fear that life without her lover will be intolerably isolated, and the violent partner may play upon those fears to keep her in the relationship. In order to overcome this obstacle, the woman who is battered may have to settle questions of her lesbian identity and to decide to what extent she will remain closeted before she can consider separating.

If two lesbians have more or less the same physical and material resources, and both are violent, they may not believe the assaults are really battering or really violence, simply because they both participate in it. Point out that violence by both partners doesn't mean there is no problem, but rather that there are two people with problems. Try to focus, in the group, on the idea that each person is responsible for her own violence. Self-blame will obscure the fact that the woman is being assaulted and preserve the misleading idea that if she would stop her violence, her partner would, too. There is no guarantee that if one partner stops, the other will, too. In addition, if a woman has not yet been able to control her violence to her partner, there may not be any reason to believe that circumstances will change soon, and meanwhile, she is *still* in danger from her retaliating partner.

As mentioned above, heterosexual women, who have experienced assault only from men, may assume they are safe in a women's group. Lesbians, who have been hit by other women, may not feel so safe. If a group member describes her own assaultive behavior, you'll need to be particularly alert to signs of fear or anger in other group members. You may need to ask directly how everyone is feeling and to help participants describe their feelings, being careful to guide participants away from putting down the woman who admits to her own violence. (If this occurs in a mixed group, heterosexual women may express their fear and anger in terms of homophobia or stereotyping remarks about lesbians, and you will have to state immediately that such reactions are not supportive and not acceptable.)

The Need for a Special Group

The time may come when lesbians and heterosexual women who are battered will mix well in groups and learn from each other. However, heterosexuals have enough false assumptions and fears about lesbians, and lesbians are understandably fearful enough about the homophobia of heterosexuals, that neither should have to grapple with those feelings when they're already in crisis. There is a great need for groups, shelters and other services for lesbians who are battered. So if you have expertise about battering, find out whether lesbian organizations in your community are providing services related to battering, and offer to exchange information or services with them. If you do become involved in organizing a group, don't forget that many lesbians are mothers, and do everything you can to provide childcare.

Lesbian groups should be led by lesbians, or if there are two leaders, at least one should be a lesbian. In many respects the groups will be similar to groups for heterosexual women. However, discussions of patriarchy and power differentials between men and women will probably take a different form, possibly centering, for instance, on whether or not lesbian violence grows out of the heterosexual models of our predominantly heterosexual society. There is a wide range of opinion on this question, and as leaders you need not have the definitive answer. Discussion of this and other new and difficult questions can provide tentative answers for some women, while reassuring others that they aren't at fault for not knowing the answers. You may also want to discuss the emotional abuse and physical assaults of lesbians by individuals and institutions, sanctioned by the predominant heterosexual society.

If you're responsible for the formation of a lesbian group and have read through this book to choose exercises or topics, notice the specific references to heterosexual relationships, and consider whether you might modify the exercises for your own use. If you have doubts about their usefulness, discuss your doubts with the group. We believe all the exercises are pertinent to lesbians involved with violent partners. Lesbians, for instance, may be subjected to a cycle of violence and be "brainwashed"; they may lose sight of their most valued traits and experience loss and grief. Although there are important differences between lesbians' and heterosexuals' situations, and in some of their feelings and attitudes, there are many commonalities as well. Those of us who work with lesbians and heterosexuals who abuse and are abused are just beginning to make some guesses about which are which. We hope that group members and leaders will encourage each other to explore the ramifications of both differences and similarities.

Second Phase Groups

Although some women attend drop-in groups for many weeks or months after they've separated from an abusive man, most women find the instability of attendance and the crisis situations of participants too distressing to want to continue for very long. After about six weeks, many women wish they could work on problems beyond the critical questions about staying or leaving, but they hesitate to take group time for their problems when others are in immediate danger or distress.

Second phase groups are designed for women who have been away from the abusive man for at least six weeks, and who want to make a commitment to a weekly group. Members usually want to work on issues of fear, custody, loneliness, developing assertiveness, dating new men, finding adequate paid work and making friends. The content may be like that of support groups, therapy, or consciousness-raising groups. We think second phase groups work best if they combine some of the activities and advantages of all those kinds of groups. The group format can change as the members change, move into new situations and face new problems.

Because the women in second phase groups are usually not in crisis, they may be more willing than drop-in group members to participate actively in decision-making about the format. It's important to provide flexibility of format so that each woman feels free to take more responsibility as she recovers from the damage of the abusive man. There may be wide variation among participants in their rate of recovery, depending on the length of the relationship, the intensity of the abuse, age and a host of other factors.

Although some women recover from the consequences of abuse with little help from professionals or other structured support, others need multifaceted assistance over a period of months or years. Don't be surprised if some are still wrestling with basic problems of how to make friends or how to manage financial decisions several years after the abusive relationship has ended. Often women may take years to break the pattern of chronic crisis, either because they haven't learned to protect themselves from chaotic relationships and economic emergencies, or because those stressful situations are perpetuated by the former partner's harassment for months or years after the separation. In many instances illness, poverty, traumatized children and shattered family relationships are the legacy of the man who battered, and the problems accompanying these situations take years to repair, or to learn to live with.

Those who participate in second phase groups sometimes feel the greatest need for support and intimacy, and yet they often have the most fear of trusting anyone. This ambivalence may result in reaching out to others in the group, and then either withdrawing in fear, or suspecting the other person of rejection or hostility.

Women in second phase groups may be less eager to exchange or use each other's telephone numbers than those in drop-in groups. In a drop-in group a woman who has reached out to another may find she doesn't care to spend time with the other participant, after all. In that case, if she stays away from the group for a few weeks there is a good chance the other woman will be gone. In a second phase group each woman is expected to attend each week, and if things don't work out well between two women who have spent time outside the group, it may be embarrassing to face each other in the group. For this reason, members should be given the option to call each other, but also encouraged to go a little more slowly if they have doubts about how it will work out.

Often these groups continue for two or three years with very little change in membership. A close bond develops whether or not the women see each other outside of regular group meetings. This kind of group can develop into a sort of substitute family for a woman who takes a long time to rebuild her social network and family structure.

The Group of Two*

It isn't always possible, of course, to form a group of even a few women who have similar interests, situations or difficulties,

---

* Only one of the co-authors has used this approach; the other two have concerns about confidentiality and intrusiveness. We share this model for your consideration, in view of your own style and ethical concerns.

in addition to having been battered. In some communities women feel especially isolated from people who can listen and help. Perhaps these women can't get to the group because of its timing or location, or they hesitate to go because they feel they are too "different" from the others. However, they may be willing to talk on the telephone or in person to someone they perceive as similar to them.

If you know two women who have some important things in common, whether they attend a group or not, you can try to get them together as a "Group of Two." Ask each woman whether you can describe her situation and interests to the other and ask if each is willing to call the other. You needn't relate anything private, except that each has been battered, and something they have in common. The important thing is to be sure each person is clear about what is all right for you to disclose to the other. When you have permission from each, say something like this: "Mary, I talked to Sue, the woman I thought might like to get together with you. I told her you're in your fifties, like theatre and would like to know someone who has been through abuse and who'd like to go to a play once in a while. She's interested in meeting you and asked me to give you her number. She'd like to have your number as well. Can I tell her you'll call?"

Mary and Sue, of course, may be quite shy about contacting each other. That's one of the risks you take. Perhaps neither of them will call, or they may need a little coaxing from you, before they're willing. If they never do get in touch with each other, you've put in a little time with no positive result, but no harm is done either. It's surprising how often even shy women *are* willing to call. There is no way to predict who will follow through until you try it.

Another method is to ask if Mary and Sue would like to meet each other in your office. When they arrive, talk with them informally, ask them to tell each other a little about their situations, what they're afraid of, what they'd like to have happen in their lives. Then, using your judgment about how relaxed they are with each other, end the session after twenty minutes or so, and ask if they'd like to continue their conversation over coffee.

Once the women do get together the results are out of your hands. They may become friends for years and years, or they may not get along at all. Or one may give the impression of not being interested in pursuing the relationship, so that the second woman has hurt feelings. That may present a new problem, and you'll be tempted, perhaps, to blame yourself. However, rejection and the fear of it are major problems for anyone who's been isolated for a long period. This may turn out to be the best time and circumstance to develop ways to cope with it, especially if you can give the woman ongoing support or therapy.

It may be much easier for the woman to get through the risk of being rejected or the reality of it when she has you as a support person to talk to about it. Since you know both people, you may even be able to make some guesses about why it's happening. In any case, it's the beginning of relearning how to reach out to people and how to trust those who are trustworthy. You'll be there to remind the woman that if the goal she wants doesn't work out, that isn't necessarily her fault.

If the rejection does have something to do with the way she is behaving, you can use the opportunity to help her realize it may be the result of long years of emotional abuse, virtual imprisonment, or chronic fear and insecurity, which has affected how she relates to everyone. She has learned to cope with a terrifying situation, and now she needs to develop other ways to handle new situations. With your help she can relinquish the outmoded skills and substitute others.

The key to all these groups is ending isolation. Each provides the opportunity for women to know they're not alone in being abused, but goes a step farther in enabling women to see that there are other abused women who are like them in significant ways. These are the first important steps in making changes.

Notes

1. Karen Susan Brockopp, Esther Ruth Chew, and Nona Kathryn O'Keefe, *A Descriptive Study Surveying the Frequency and Severity of Intra-Couple Dating Violence at the High School Level*, Ph.D. thesis. For more information write to: Esther Chew, P.O. Box 161356, Sacramento, CA 95816.

2. Ginny NiCarthy, "Addictive Love and Abuse: A Course for Teenage Women," in Sue Davidson, ed., *The Second Mile: Contemporary Approaches in Counseling Young Women*(Tucson: New Directions for Young Women, 1983), pp. 115–159. Available from New Directions for Young Women, 312 S. Washington, Seattle, WA 98104.

3. See *Every Day a New Beginning* (Center City, MN: Hazelden Foundation, Box 176, Center City, MN 55012, 1982) and Ginny NiCarthy, *Getting Free: A Handbook for Women in Abusive Relationships* (Seattle: Seal Press, 1982).

4. See "Lesbian Task Force Conference Report," *NCADV Voice,* January 1984 (Washington, D.C.: National Coaliation Against Domestic Violence, 1500 Massachusetts Avenue NW, #35, Washington, D.C. 20005), p. 8.

Articles on this topic periodically appear in *Off Our Backs* (1841 Columbia Road NW, Room #212, Washington, D.C. 20009), *Gay Community News* (167 Tremont Street, Boston, MA 02111), and *Plexus* (545 Athol Avenue, Oakland, CA 94606).

Chapter 12

Preventing Burnout: Enjoying Group Leadership

The challenges of leading groups for abused women are many, as are the rewards. The focus of this final chapter will be on doing preventive work to decrease the problem of burnout and on increasing the rewards of leadership.

Leading groups for women who've been abused is demanding as well as exciting, because the stakes are high and the clear victories few and far between. It's difficult for leaders to maintain emotional distance from the issues raised in the group, since most of us have experienced at least the threat of sexual or physical violence at some point in our own lives.

It's hard for leaders to leave a group each week wondering whether the members will be alive or unharmed the next week, or if they'll choose to return to the group. And no one can ever know when a vindictive batterer may successfully track down a woman or her children, even after she has left and gone into hiding from him.

This is stressful work, so burnout is a threat to everyone who works with battered women. If you are leading groups in addition to doing a full-time job (in or out of the home), the risk of burnout is particularly high, given the stress that results from competing demands for your time and energy.

Understanding and Avoiding Burnout

The term burnout was first used a decade ago by Dr. Herbert Freudenberger to describe the cumulative debilitating effects of chronic and severe job-related stress.[1]

Hans Selye, one of the writers to identify and explore the importance of stress and its management, defined stress as the general response of the body to any demand made upon it.[2] The causes of stress may be internal or external, psychological, physical or social. Stress can be energizing or debilitating, depending on your response. Since some stress is necessary for a productive life, the minimization of distress is a more useful goal than total elimination of stress.

The body responds to stress with a variety of chemical reactions which produce both physical and mental changes. In crisis situations, people may need this push to survive by "fight or flight." Unfortunately, sometimes neither response is possible when complex solutions are needed. So instead of a short-term state of physiological alertness, which is useful for emergency situations, the body is often exposed to chronic physiological overactivity caused by stress. If the body doesn't return regularly enough to its normal baseline level of activity, stress-related disorders may result, such as high blood pressure, irritability, migraine headaches and lower-back pain.

The effects of prolonged chronic stress vary widely among individuals. Sex, age, family history, economic status and genetic predisposition all influence the effects of stress, as do various coping strategies and an individual's overall state of health. However, everyone has limits.

Since there is always more to do than is possible in working with battered women, many leaders are tempted to try to do the impossible. In the process, they often push themselves beyond their threshold, with the result that they accomplish less rather than more. This process is not only personally destructive but also interferes with their work.

Symptoms

The symptoms of burnout often cluster in the following three categories:
Emotional and physical exhaustion
You may experience lethargy and fatigue, especially as the time to lead the group approaches, or you may feel too drained for your post-group discussion with your co-leader, only to find yourself unable to sleep. And when you have slept, you awaken feeling exhausted. Physical complaints often emerge and intensify: chronic colds, insomnia, stomach problems, tension headaches and neck or shoulder strain are common.

Disillusionment

Excitement and satisfaction about doing a good and necessary job fade from view. You become irritable, anxious or vaguely depressed. You may crack an occasional joke about your ineffectiveness in working with battered women. These are early signs of burnout, which need attention. If you don't examine their meaning, the jokes and irritability, for instance, may develop into a habit of using derogatory labels or cynical humor when discussing group members with your co-leader. These increased negative feelings about the group diminish your effectiveness as a leader. Your awareness of your diminished effectiveness adds to your sense of disillusionment, which is highly contagious to participants, your co-leader and other agency personnel. You may find excuses to miss the group more and more frequently. You may also find yourself returning to or increasing your use of tobacco, alcohol, drugs or food.

Self-doubt and blame

Self-doubt often results from the cumulative effects of exhaustion and disillusionment. You may feel that you're performing mechanically, like a robot, both in and outside of the group. This contrasts sadly with your faded memory of your initial excitement and previously increasing effectiveness in working with battered women. You hide your feelings out of shame, never realizing that many other leaders have felt this way, thus adding to your stress and increasing your isolation.

The following list of behavioral signs can be a useful way to check your symptoms against those common to the syndrome we today call burnout.[3]

Psychological and Physiological Symptoms of Burnout

- Headaches and muscle tension
- Depression/boredom/apathy
- Absenteeism/decline in performance
- Hypertension/insomnia
- Irritability/increased anxiety
- Increase in smoking, drinking, drug dependency and other addictions
- Escape activities, such as shopping sprees, daydreaming or overeating
- Stress-related physical and emotional ailments
- Tension with family and/or friends

Causes

In addition to pinpointing the symptoms of burnout, it is also important to recognize its various causes, differentiating between those that are present in our society, the job itself, and each individual.

Societal Influences

There are numerous ways in which our economic system and cultural values contribute to each individual's potential for burnout. The following are important societal contributors to stress:

- the fear of nuclear destruction
- the fast pace of life in urban, technological centers
- increased mobility, which has undermined lasting support systems and a sense of belonging to a particular community
- the myth of the "superwoman" created by women's changing roles in the workforce, contrasted with the predominence of low-wage, dead-end jobs for women
- the escalation of unemployment, particularly in minority communities
- increased alienation from our work because of automation and specialization
- racism
- sexism
- homophobia

Any of these external constraints may be sapping your energy and hopefulness and increasing your level of stress. Realizing which ones affect you helps to decrease self-blame for the stress you feel. You may also want to increase your sense of power and optimism by joining others who are working to change certain aspects of our society.

In addition, the profit-based nature of our economy may distort a group leader's evaluation of her work. Constant emphasis in the media on material success glorifies the small percentage of wealthy citizens and corporations who dominate the country by knowing how to "profit" from opportunity—that is, taking from any interaction more than they've contributed to it.

The resulting economic inequality is obscured by an ideology that assumes that all people who work hard will be equally successful and rewarded. The corollary of this belief teaches that those who are less successful economically are failures, lazy, or personally flawed in some way that is their own, individual fault. In fact, the capitalist system presupposes an economic pyramid, and very few people can ever be at the top—most people must, by definition, remain at its base.

In this country there is further stratification of that economic pyramid, based on power differentials between men and women and between whites and people of color. Social institutions formalize these power differentials, along with that between rich and poor. So the economic deck is heavily stacked against the likelihood of success for women, people of color and poor people. And those who hold onto the expectation of equal opportunity for all may blame themselves for the failures of the system.

You may find yourself doing that when some things don't go well with the group. Because you're a woman working on behalf of women, many of whom are poor (partly because they can't get access to family income), you may slip into the idea that your personal failings are responsible for your inability to accomplish as much as is needed.

In fact, the problem is more likely to be that you're underpaid and your agency is underfunded and understaffed because you're doing "women's work." You're probably not able to take the time between group sessions to do really adequate referrals. Even if you had that time, neither public nor private funding is available to provide sufficient backup services for the women you would refer. It's essential to remember that although you're working on a problem that is faced by individuals, it is a social, political and economic problem that cannot be resolved individually.

If the problem of violence against women is to be solved, it must be worked at collectively, and it is important for those who are working on it to become both realistic and politically aware. Abused women benefit from talking and listening to each other, which helps them recognize that what they endure is part of a fundamental social problem and is not their fault. Group leaders benefit from talking and listening to each other, which helps them remember that they're part of a political movement designed to change the power distribution in society. They remind each other that the work with individual women is important and that it must be backed up with legal, social and political change. Just as women who are battered must develop the hope that they can change and gain control over their lives, group leaders must believe that over time, and working with other women, they can change the power dynamics of society.[4]

Your Work

In evaluating the causes of burnout, also pay attention to the ways in which this particular work affects you. Inadequate preparation and training can easily lead to unrealistic expectations and, therefore, to early disappointment. The life-threatening nature of physical abuse provokes urgency and often a high level of anxiety and stress in participants, which is easily communicated to group leaders. Inadequate funding for community agencies geared to issues of abuse is often passed on to leaders in the form of inadequate or no salary. Hostility from those who deny the existence of the abuse of women can leave you vulnerable to stress. Consider other particular factors that may well be contributing to burnout, such as a conservative political climate in the community, competitiveness between professionals and paraprofessionals, intense racial tension between two or more groups, or geographic isolation. Ask yourself whether you want to work to change these negative influences or if you are willing just to acknowledge their effects on you at this time.

Group leaders sometimes feel they can't stop the work they're doing, even when burnout is threatening their own physical and emotional well-being. Leaders are often afraid that women will die, fall apart emotionally or return to physically or emotionally abusive relationships if the leader decides to leave her position. They tell themselves that no one else would be willing or qualified to do this work. Abused women express similar concerns about leaving the abuser.

There may well be truth in these fears, as there are in the fears of battered women. But this is probably only partial truth. Generally, someone else *will* come forward to lead an already established group, especially if you offer her some training before you depart. Begin by approaching women you would like to see replace you and discuss the exciting as well as the difficult aspects of the job. Then, if necessary, send announcements of the anticipated opening for the position of group leader to shelters, community agencies and private practitioners.

If no one appropriate comes forth to replace you, you will need to ask yourself if you can afford to be the *only* person in your community willing to do this work. A burned-out leader presents a poor model to battered women. Whether you decide to leave the group, to reduce stress in other areas of your life or to increase your coping skills so that you can stay, remember that you must avoid becoming an abused group leader.

Yourself

Finally, there are numerous causes of burnout that may be traced directly to the leader herself. Individual tolerance for stress varies, as do the mechanisms each person develops for coping. A "Type A" behavior pattern often results in an individual's taking on more stress than she or he can physiologically handle.[5] Type A people are generally driven, ambitious, aggressive, competitive and eager to get things done. They often feel themselves racing anxiously with the clock to accomplish the many tasks they set for themselves each day. There is some relationship to the Wonder Woman syndrome (see page 76). By contrast, Type B people are less competitive and achievement-oriented, more easygoing and relatively unconcerned about time.

An unhealthy diet or lifestyle can also undermine your tolerance for stress, as can an inadequate support system. Perfectionism and a tendency to self-blame can exacerbate burnout. (See *Getting Free* by Ginny NiCarthy, or David Burns' book, *Feeling Good*, for strategies for dealing with self-criticism.[6]) Individuals' responses to stress will also vary with other life events.

Having identified the symptoms and causes of burnout, you are now in a better position to do preventative or corrective work to minimize its effect on your ability to lead groups for women who've been abused. Techniques that people have found useful for dealing with stress and burnout include:

- biofeedback
- relaxation and imagery
- progressive relaxation
- hypnosis
- meditation
- yoga
- massage
- vigorous exercise
- time management
- vacations
- thought-stopping and cognitive restructuring

The remainder of this chapter details some other approaches we've found useful.

Networking and Support

Sharing with Your Co-Leader

You and your co-leader can help each other focus on the long view and the slow unfolding of change by remembering that women often need to leave an abusive man many times before they finally stay away for good. Compliment each other on the good and difficult work you're doing together. Remind each other that you are part of a worldwide network of women who are working to help reduce battering and its effects.

Sharing with Your Partner and Friends

Let your friends, including an intimate partner if you have one, know why you've chosen to do this work. Tell them of your goals and expectations, and share your frustration with them. Invite them to tell you when they don't want to hear any more. Don't expect them to read your mind; they need specific information about how to help you persevere.

You might want to structure some quiet time for unwinding after you and your co-leader have reviewed the meeting and finished plans for the next one. Or you may prefer to immerse yourself in physical activity or in playing with children or pets to distract yourself. If you include any friends in this process of unwinding, tell them if you want a hug, a ready ear, some advice, a cold lemonade or a cup of tea. The most important issue here is to take some control over this post-group time, rather than feeling still controlled by emotions aroused in the group.

Cultivating Pleasure and Competency

It's important to have other, more predictable, sources of pleasure and competency in your life, beyond leading these groups. Even though you will feel rewards in response to the group, they will often come infrequently and when least expected. It's important to know that you can count on feelings of pleasure and satisfaction in other ways. Perhaps you like to paint, run, repair bicycles, or you're good at volleyball or bowling. Maybe your everyday work provides you with a sense of accomplishment and satisfaction. Review your life for situations in which you feel pleasure and competency. Add activities which provide those pleasant feelings if you're not experiencing them often enough. And let the group provide them as a bonus when possible.

Self-Care and Pleasure

Practice the kind of good preventive self-care that you recommend to others: adequate rest, good nutrition, pleasurable social contacts, and regular vigorous exercise. Caring for yourself will increase your own well-being and allow you to model these activities for the group members. You can brag about your efforts at the beginning of the group, from time to time.

If you're beginning to feel stretched too thin, carefully consider whether you're willing to give up something else in order to continue leading a group. Reflect on your history and rate yourself on how well you're usually able to pace yourself. Take note if you have often taken on one task too many and then retreated from everything for a while after burning out. It may take some experimentation, but attempt to establish a balance in your life between work and play, between giving and receiving, between activities that demand much of you and those that replenish your personal and political resources.

Limit-Setting and Boundaries

Women who've been battered often have intense and immediate needs of many different kinds. At times you'll be tempted to take one of the women in the group home with you. Don't! But between that extreme and the other (of never seeing or talking to participants outside of the group) lies a wide range of options for having contact with some or all of the group members outside of the group setting. The realities of your own life, the other options in your community open to abused women, your values and stamina will all influence the limits you set with the group participants. We recommend your giving consideration to the following three areas in which you'll need to set some limits: guarding your time; setting personal boundaries; and seeing group members for individual counseling.

Guarding Your Time

Helping women recognize and decide whether to leave battering relationships can easily dominate your life. For a while, you may find yourself wanting to read everything that's ever been written about abusive relationships and unable to discuss anything else. It's important to educate yourself and others on this topic, but no matter what you do, the problem won't go away soon. Pace yourself so that you can work steadily for a long time, rather than burning out quickly. Find a rhythm that enhances your life, rather than one that takes over your life.

You'll also want to limit in some way the time that you spend on the group itself. If necessary, group sessions can be shortened somewhat to accommodate your need to talk afterwards with your co-leader, to unwind and to still get to sleep at night. Consultation with your co-leader might feel rewarding, rather than draining, if you meet regularly for dinner or lunch. Notice feelings of resentment or balance in yourself when you think about the group and then consider whether you're giving too much or too little time to the group. If you've felt hurried by or distant from your co-leader or the group, giving a bit more time, energy or thought to the group might help reduce tension you have about the group.

Setting Personal Boundaries

Monitor your desire to play mother, daughter, spiritual leader, martyr or superwoman with participants. The task of group leadership is a demanding one. The group time may be all you can give, in order to save some energy for your other regular activities. Or you may want to make exceptions to this and spend some telephone time with some participants. But if you give out your phone number, expect to be called at the wrong time (for you) with an important crisis (for her). How and where will you then draw the limit of your involvement? There's no pat answer, but be very thoughtful about this. It's okay *not* to give out a personal or work phone number, but be sure to make other numbers available to group members, such as the phone numbers of crisis centers and other community resources that are responsive to abused women.

In general it's preferable to start with little or no out-of-group contact than to extend yourself too far to a group member and later pull back. This pulling back will probably be experienced as rejection by the participant at a time when she may be particularly vulnerable. Remember that participants need to develop a support system that extends beyond the batterers and the group leaders. They need to explore appropriate social service agencies on their own or with the help of another group member. Mutual support will help them learn to trust their own capabilities, rather than becoming overly dependent on another powerful person (you) as they move away from the abuser.

Seeing Group Members for Individual Counseling

If you are a counselor in an agency or in private practice, you'll want to develop a general position on whether or not you'll see group members for individual counseling in that other setting. Careful attention must be paid to several ethical concerns. The group should *never* be, or appear to be, a recruiting ground for your agency or private practice. It's important to provide several names of possible appropriate counselors if you're asked for referrals.

Sooner or later it will become apparent in the group that you have a special relationship with those participants that you're counseling individually. This should then be acknowledged openly. A participant may feel a need to have other group members know of her special individual relationship with a leader. She may, for example, become more open, controlling, overly helpful, or rejecting of other members. As a result, the other members may feel rejected, jealous, respectful, inferior in status, superior (because *they* don't need individual counseling, too) or neutral. Any feelings that other group members may have about this special relationship should be discussed openly at the time the participant demonstrates or describes your dual relationship.

Maintaining confidentiality about what's said in individual sessions is an important responsibility of the counselor who sees a battered woman both in a group and individually. Another important issue to consider before agreeing to see the participant individually is whether you are the best person or agency you know to work with her. Many abused women have histories of incest and childhood emotional abuse, as well as a vulnerability to current or past drug or alcohol abuse, and they may do best working with therapists who are specialists in these fields. Think carefully about the optimum setting and expertise that can be provided for each participant before you accept her as an individual client. It's best to accept only one or two participants as clients at first. Then you can evaluate whether you are able to see clients in multiple settings responsibly, rather than over-extending yourself and then pulling back.

If you become known in your community as a counselor with expertise in working individually with abused women (in either a community agency or in a private practice), you may also face the opposite dilemma: referring an individual client of yours to the group you lead. We believe that most battered women need the supportive environment that exists in a group.

But we also know from experience just how difficult it can be to convince an isolated, fearful woman to join a group, even when her counselor will be one of the leaders. Nonetheless, we strongly recommend telling each abused woman you see in your private or agency practice about the group, unless she is too disturbed to participate. (See the section in Chapter 8 on working in the group with particularly distressed women.) Then leave the decision to her about whether or not to attend.

Reevaluating Personal Goals

Periodically review the personal goals you originally wrote for yourself when you began leading the group. We suggest a review every three months.

Leaders often experience quite a bit of disruption in their daily lives during the first few weeks of leading a group for abused women. This may interfere with meeting many of their goals during the first three months. If this happens, reevaluate your goals at that three-month mark. You needn't be alarmed if you initially experience some sleeplessness, anxiety and nightmares after the group session and possibly the following night. The day after group may be dominated by memories of participants' stories and situations.

Your awareness of the participants' experiences may also result in some or all of the following reactions:

1. A heightened awareness of the physical and emotional dangers inherent to women in this society (such as rape, incest, physical and emotional abuse)
2. Anger toward men in general and offenders of all kinds in particular
3. Suspicion of, or distance from, any man with whom you are currently involved
4. Increased feeling of helplessness about your own ability to end or decrease battering
5. Generalized fear

Feelings noted in numbers 2 through 5 above typically diminish after the first month or two of leading a group. If they remain after three to six months, evaluate any particular aspect of your own life or group situation that might be aggravating these natural initial reactions.

If after six to nine months your goals aren't being met, you might want to think again about any changes that can be made. If you have a consultant, such as a close colleague or a supervisor, it might help to include her (or him) in this decision process. Listen to her or his evaluation of the skills you've gained and the skills you need to work on. Were your initial goals and expectations unrealistically high? Are you being too self-critical as a result? Might your feelings shift toward staying if you could be working to build these missing skills? Your consultant may be able to help you see themes or patterns in your complaints over time. These patterns may help you determine whether the problems are correctible or not. Also keep your co-leader posted about your thinking and ask for her views. But remember, the final decision to leave or stay is your own—just as it is for the women who've been abused.

If you're quite dissatisfied and you see no way to improve the situation, you might want to think about finding a replacement for yourself as co-leader if things don't improve soon. Maybe you just don't function well working with a drop-in group; it can be very frustrating. Or perhaps working with women who've been abused touches off some old wounds of your own that you want to bury again or to heal in some counseling for yourself. Maybe you're terrific in one-to-one situations but find you don't function well as a group leader.

There are many reasons to do this work and just as many to move on, if it's not for you after all. But if you decide to leave, do so responsibly. Let the group know well in advance (a month or two) when you'll be leaving. Reassure them repeatedly that this is a *personal* decision. Do your best to insure that the participants don't blame themselves for your departure. Obviously you can't control their thoughts, but you can be sensitive to the tendency of women who've been abused to consider themselves responsible for the actions of others.

Final Thoughts

We assume that leading a group for women who've been abused will stir your creative processes, just as it has ours. As you find yourself creating your own structure and inventing exercises, consider discussing them with other people who lead groups. Organizing discussion groups at conferences on violence against women and writing articles for newsletters or journals such as *Aegis* are some ways to share the wealth of material and expertise that women are creating. We won't have to keep reinventing the wheel if we exchange our new knowledge with each other.

We hope that this book will be part of that process of information sharing. The following bibliography also provides other sources of information beyond the scope of this book. Like any reference book, we hope ours will provide you with a viewpoint and a structure that enables you to begin. Then your own variations on the themes will evolve. Writing this book collectively has forced us to articulate our differences, as well as our commonly held beliefs. We've described some of these differences in this book, and compromised on many more in the process of writing and rewriting. In many ways, this mirrors the process of compromise and articulation of similarities and differences that has marked our years together as co-leaders. We invite you to join us in this process.

Notes

1. Herbert Freudenberger, *Burn Out: The High Cost of High Achievement* (New York: Doubleday & Company, 1980).

2. Hans Selye, *Stress Without Distress* (New York: Signet, 1974).

3. Paula Jorde, *Avoiding Burnout: Strategies for Managing Time, Space and People in Early Childhood Education* (Washington, D.C.: Acropolis Books, 1982).

4. See Barbara J. Hart's article, "Burn-Out: A Political View," in *Aegis*, no. 32, Autumn 1981, pp. 35–40.

5. Meyer Friedman and Ray Rosenman, *Type A Behavior and Your Heart* (New York: Fawcett Crest, 1974).

6. See David Burns, *Feeling Good* (New York: Sigret, 1980) and Ginny NiCarthy, *Getting Free: A Handbook for Women in Abusive Relationships* (Seattle: Seal Press, 1982).

Suggested Readings
and Resources

The following list of books, articles, journals, and organizations are selected resources for those working with abused women and for abused women themselves. The list is arranged by topic. The length of suggested readings reflects the exciting growth of literature in recent years about battering and related issues. Obviously, there is still much to be written, especially for women of color, lesbians, disabled women, religious women, older women and teen-aged women in abusive relationships. We are unable to present an exhaustive reading list, but we hope it will provide the reader with useful resources for continually augmenting her or his knowledge of these important topics.

Battering

Books

Armstrong, Louise. *The Home Front: Notes from the Family War Zone.* New York: McGraw-Hill, 1983.

Battered Women: Issues of Public Policy. A Consultation Sponsored by the United States Commission on Civil Rights, Washington, D.C., January 30–31, 1978.

Bowker, Lee H. *Beating Wife-Beating.* Lexington, MA: Lexington Books (Heath), 1983.

Brockopp, Karen Susan, Esther Ruth Chew, and Nona Kathryn O'Keeffe. *A Descriptive Study Surveying the Frequency and Severity of Intra-Couple Dating Violence at the High School Level.* Ph.D. thesis. For more information write to: Esther Chew, P.O. Box 161356, Sacramento, CA 95816.

Dobash, R. Emerson and Russell Dobash. *Violence Against Wives: A Case Against the Patriarchy.* New York: Free Press (Macmillan), 1979.

Fleming, Jennifer Baker. *Stopping Wife Abuse: A Guide to the Emotional, Psychological, and Legal Implications for the Abused Woman and Those Helping Her.* New York: Anchor Press/Doubleday, 1979.

Fortune, Marie. *Sexual Violence: The Unmentionable Sin: An Ethical and Pastoral Perspective.* New York: Pilgrim Press, 1983.

Fortune, Marie and Denise Hormann. *Family Violence: A Workshop Manual for Clergy and Other Service Providers.* Seattle: The Center for the Prevention of Sexual and Domestic Violence, 1980. Available from The Center for the Prevention of Sexual and Domestic Violence, 1914 North 34th, #205, Seattle, WA 98103.

Freeman, M. D. A. *Violence in the Home: A Socio-Legal Study.* Westmead, Hampshire: Gower, 1980.

Giles-Sims, Jean. *Wife Battering: A Systems Theory Approach.* New York: Guilford Press, 1983.

Kim, Bok-Lim C., et al. *Women in Shadows: A Handbook for Service Providers Working with Asian Wives of U.S. Military Personnel.* La Jolla, CA: National Committee Concerned with Asian Wives of U.S. Servicemen, 1981. Available from the National Committee Concerned with Asian Wives of U.S. Servicemen, 964 La Jolla Rancho Road, La Jolla, CA 92037.

Martin, Del. *Battered Wives.* Revised edition. San Francisco: Volcano Press (Dept. B, 330 Ellis Street, San Francisco, CA 94102), 1981.

McNulty, Faith. *The Burning Bed: The True Story of an Abused Wife.* New York: Bantam Books, 1981.

National Center on Women and Family Law, Inc. *Legal Advocacy for Battered Women.* New York: National Center on Women and Family Law, Inc., 1982. Available from NCOWFL, 799 Broadway, Room 402, New York, NY 10003.

NiCarthy, Ginny. *Getting Free: A Handbook for Women in Abusive Relationships.* Seattle: Seal Press, 1982.

Pagelow, Mildred Daley. *Family Violence.* New York: Praeger, forthcoming in 1984.

Pagelow, Mildred Daley. *Woman-Battering: Victims and their Experiences.* Beverly Hills, CA: Sage Publications, 1981.

Roberts, Albert R. *Battered Women and their Families: Intervention Strategies and Treatment Programs.* New York: Springer Pub. Co., 1984.

Roy, Maria, editor. *The Abusive Partner: An Analysis of Domestic Battering.* New York: Van Nostrand Reinhold, 1982.

Russell, Diana E. H. *Rape in Marriage.* New York: Macmillan Pub. Co., 1982.

Schechter, Susan. *Women and Male Violence: The Visions and Struggles of the Battered Women's Movement.* Boston: South End Press, 1982.

Sonkin, Daniel Jay and Michael Durphy. *Learning to Live Without Violence: A Handbook for Men.* San Francisco: Volcano Press (Dept. B, 330 Ellis Street, San Francisco, CA 94102), 1982.

Stacey, William A. and Anson Shupe. *The Family Secret: Domestic Violence in America.* Boston: Beacon Press, 1983.

Stark, Evan, Anne Flitcraft, and William Frazier. *Wife Abuse in the Medical Setting.* Rockville, MD: National Clearinghouse on Domestic Violence, 1981. Available on a loan basis for $5.00 from the Lending Library of the Center for Women Policy Studies, 2000 P Street NW, Washington, D.C. 20036.

Straus, Murray A., Richard J. Gelles and Suzanne K. Steinmetz. *Behind Closed Doors: Violence in the American Family.* New York: Anchor Press/Doubleday, 1980.

Vapnar, Gretchen S. *The Shelter Experience: A Guide to Shelter Organization and Management for Groups Working Against Domestic Violence.* Rockville, MD: National Clearinghouse on Family Violence, 1980. Available on a loan basis for $5.00 from the Lending Library of the Center for Women Policy Studies, 2000 P Street NW, Washington, D.C. 20036.

Walker, Lenore E. *The Battered Woman.* New York: Harper & Row, 1979.

Warrior, Betsy. *Battered Women's Directory* (Eighth Edition). Cambridge, MA: Betsy Warrior, 1982. Available from Battered Women's Directory, Women's Education Center, 46 Pleasant Street, Cambridge, MA 02139.

White, Evelyn C. *Chain Chain Change: For Black Women Dealing with Physical and Emotional Abuse.* Seattle: Seal Press, forthcoming in 1985.

Zambrano, Myrna J. *Mejor Sola Que Mal Acompañada: Para la Mujer Golpeada/For the Latina in an Abusive Relationship.* Seattle: Seal Press, forthcoming in 1985.

Articles and Pamphlets

Bernard, M. L. and J. L. Bernard. "Violent intimacy: The family as a model for love relationships." *Family Relations: Journal of Applied Family and Child Statistics,* 1983 (Volume 32, Number 2), pp. 283–286.

Breines, Wini and Linda Gordon. "The New Scholarship on Family Violence." *Signs,* Vol. 8, No. 3, Spring 1983, pp. 490–531.

Deming, Barbara. *On Anger/New Men, New Women: Some Thoughts on Non-Violence.* Philadelphia: New Society Publishers, 1982.

Ferraro, Kathleen J. and John M. Johnson, "How women experience battering: The process of victimization." *Social Problems,* 1983 (Volume 9, Number 3), pp. 325–339.

For Shelter and Beyond: An Educational Manual for Working with Women Who Are Battered. Boston: Massachusetts Coalition of Battered Women's Service Groups, 1981. Available from MCBWSG, 25 West Street, Fifth Floor, Boston, MA 02111.

Marecek, Mary. *Say, "No!" to Violence: Voices of Women Who Experience Violence.* Boston: Red Sun Press, 1983.

My Neighbor is a Battered Woman. Albuquerque, NM: New Mexico Commission on the Status of Women, 1981.

NiCarthy, Ginny. "Addictive Love and Abuse: A Course for Teenage Women." *The Second Mile: Contemporary Approaches in Counseling Young Women.* Seattle: New Directions for Young Women, 1983. Available from New Directions for Young Women, 312 S. Washington, Seattle, WA 98104.

Rural Domestic Violence Intervention: A How-to-Guide. Mason City, Iowa: Crisis Intervention Service, no date.

Stark, Evan, Anne Flitcraft, and William Frazier. "Medicine and Patriarchal Violence: The Social Construction of a 'Private' Event." *International Journal of Health Sciences,* 1979 (Volume 9, Number 3).

Walker, Lenore E. "The Battered Woman Syndrome Study: Results and Discussion." In Finkelhor, D., R. Gelles, G. Hotaling, and M. Straus, *The Dark Side of Families.* Beverly Hills, CA: Sage Publishing Co., 1983.

Wilson, Carolyn and Kathryn Clarenbach. *Violence Against Women: Causes and Prevention.* A literature search and annotated bibliography published in 1979 by Women's Education Resources, Univ. of Wisconsin-Madison, 428 Lowell Hall, 610 Langdon Street, Madison, WI 53706.

Wood, Frances B. *Living Without Violence: A Community Approach to Working with Battered Women and their Children.* Fayetteville, AR: Project for Victims of Domestic Violence (Box 2915), 1981.

Journals

Aegis: The Magazine on Ending Violence Against Women. Published four times yearly by the National Communications Network, the Feminist Alliance Against Rape, and the Alliance Against Sexual Coercion, P.O. Box 21033, Washington, D.C. 20009.

Response to Violence in the Family and Sexual Assault. Published bimonthly by the Center for Women Policy Studies, 2000 P Street NW, Suite 508, Washington, D.C. 20036.

Signs: The Journal of Women in Culture and Society. Special Issue: *Women and Violence,* Volume 8, Number 3. Chicago: University of Chicago Press, 1983.

Social Work: Journal of the National Association of Social Workers. Published quarterly by the National Association of Social Workers (NASW), 7981 Eastern Avenue, Silver Spring, MD 20910.

Victimology: An International Journal. Published quarterly by Victimology, Inc., 2333 North Vernon Street, Arlington, VA 22207.

Special Issues

The selected resources we list here are intended to provide a better understanding and awareness of the many special issues related to domestic violence. In some sections, in addition to resources specifically dealing with battering, we have listed a few general anthologies we have found especially useful and important.

Women of Color

Various organizations across the country are working against battering within racial and ethnic minority communities and are writing and making video and audio tapes for their own training. We hope that such valuable resources will eventually become available on a larger scale, but at this point we have been able to find only a few materials on battering, by and for women of color, that are available to buy or to rent. The following are some general resources:

The National Coalition Against Domestic Violence (NCADV) has a Women of Color Task Force. Contact them through the NCADV national office: 1500 Massachusetts Avenue NW, Suite 35, Washington, D.C. 20005.

BIHA (Black, Indian, Hispanic & Asian) Women in Action networks with women of color nationally who are interested in or are working against family violence. They publish a newsletter and are currently putting together a library of resources and culturally specific information on domestic violence. For information, write to BIHA Women in Action, 2650 Nicollet Avenue, Minneapolis, MN 55408.

Books, Articles, Pamphlets:

American Indian Women Against Domestic Violence: Position Paper. Available from the Minnesota Coalition for Battered Women, 435 Aldine Avenue, St. Paul, MN 55104.

Axtell, Cheyla McCormack. "Building an Outreach Program." *Aegis*, 1979 (May/June), pp. 41–42.

Brooks, Anita B., Ph.D. "The Black Woman within the Program and Service Delivery Systems for Battered Women: A Cultural Response." Prepared for the Minnesota Department of Corrections, Programs and Services for Battered Women. For information write to Anita B. Bracy, c/o the Afro-American & African Studies Department, University of Minnesota, Minneapolis, MN 55455.

Cochran, Jo, J. T. Stewart, and Mayumi Tsutakawa, eds. *Gathering Ground: New Writing and Art by Northwest Women of Color*. Seattle: Seal Press, 1984.

Gómez, Alma, Cherríe Moraga, and Mariana Romo-Carmona, eds. *Cuentos: Stories by Latinas*. New York: Kitchen Table: Women of Color Press, 1983.

Joseph, Gloria I. and Jill Lewis. *Common Differences: Conflicts in Black and White Feminist Perspectives.* New York: Anchor Books/Doubleday, 1981.

Kim, Bok-Lim C. et al. *Women in Shadows: A Handbook for Service Providers Working with Asian Wives of U.S. Military Personnel.* La Jolla, CA: National Committee Concerned with Asian Wives of U.S. Servicemen, 1981. Available from the National Committee Concerned with Asian Wives of U.S. Servicemen, 964 La Jolla Rancho Road, La Jolla, CA 92037.

Moraga, Cherríe and Gloria Anzaldúa. *This Bridge Called My Back: Writings by Radical Women of Color.* New York: Kitchen Table: Women of Color Press, 1983.

Multicultural Women's Sourcebook. Women's Education Equity Act Program, 1982. Available from Education Development Center, 55 Chapel Street, Newton, MA 02160.

Pokela, Elizabeth J. "Domestic Violence: Crisis Intervention with the Hispanic Family." In *The Prevention and Treatment of Child Abuse and Neglect: A Focus on the Mexican-American Family* (Proceedings of the Second Annual Conference, San Antonio, Texas). Texas Migrant Council National Resource Center on Child Abuse and Neglect for Mexican-Americans, 1983. For information write to Texas Migrant Council, P.O. Box 2579, Laredo, TX 78044-2579.

Richie-Bush, Beth. "Facing Contradictions: Challenge for Black Feminists." *Aegis*, 1983, No. 37, pp. 14–20.

Scott, Renae. *Doing Community Outreach to Third World Women.* Boston: Domestic Violence Technical Assistance Project of Casa Myrna Vazquez, 1980.

Shaw, Linda. *Counseling the Abuse Victim.* Harrisburg: The Pennsylvania Coalition Against Domestic Violence, undated. This useful handbook has a section addressing cultural differences.

Smith, Barbara, ed. *Home Girls: A Black Feminist Anthology.* New York: Kitchen Table: Women of Color Press, 1983.

White, Evelyn C. *Chain Chain Change: For Black Women Dealing with Physical and Emotional Abuse.* Seattle: Seal Press, forthcoming in 1985.

Zambrano, Myrna M. *Mejor Sola Que Mal Acompanada: Para La Mujer Golpeada/For The Latina in an Abusive Relationship.* Seattle: Seal Press, forthcoming in 1985.

Lesbians

The Western Center on Domestic Violence (WCDV) has prepared two important resource packets: one on battering in lesbian relationships, and another on issues of homophobia and heterosexism. Both packets are available from the Center for $4.50 to WCDV members and $7.50 to non-members. Write to WCDV, 870 Market Street, Suite 1058, San Francisco, CA 94102.

The Lesbian Task Force of the National Coalition Against Domestic Violence (NCADV) is developing a lesbian battering anthology. For more information contact the NCDAV office: 1500 Massachusetts Avenue NW, Suite 35, Washington, D.C. 20005.

The Lesbian Battering Bibliography Project is also preparing an anthology of articles, resource lists and personal stories about lesbian battering. Write to them for more information: Lesbian Battering Bibliography Project, 218 Moreland Avenue, Mankato, MN 56001.

Articles on lesbian abuse periodically appear in *off our backs* (1841 Columbia Road NW, Room 212, Washington, D.C. 20009), *Gay Community News* (167 Tremont Street, Boston, MA 02111), and *Plexus* (545 Athol Avenue, Oakland, CA 94606), among other publications. Subscriptions are worthwhile.

Books, Articles, Pamphlets:

Baetz, Ruth. *Lesbian Crossroads: Personal Stories of Lesbian Struggles and Triumphs.* New York: William Morrow, 1980. Out of print, but available from the author: Ruth Baetz, 523 32nd Ave., Seattle, WA 98122.

Gay and Lesbian Social Work Practice: A Special Issue of Practice Digest. Available from the National Association of Social Workers, 7981 Eastern Avenue, Silver Spring, MD 20910.

Martin, Del. *Lesbian/Woman.* Updated and revised edition. New York: Bantam, 1984.

Moses, A. Elfin and Robert O. J. Hawkins. *Counseling Lesbian Women and Gay Men.* St. Louis: C. V. Mosby Co., 1982.

Paisley, Christine A. and Judith E. Krulewitz. "Same-Sex Assault: Sexual and Non-Sexual Violence within Lesbian Relationships." A paper presented at the National Conference of the Association for Women in Psychology, Seattle, March 1983.

Vardamis, Sharon. "Confronting Homophobia." *Aegis*, 1983, No. 37, pp. 73–77.

Disabled Women

A good resource is the Women and Disability Awareness Project, Educational Equity Concepts, Inc., 440 Park Avenue South, New York, N.Y. 10016.

The Womyn's Braille Press produces feminist and lesbian literature on tape and in Braille for women who are blind or physically disabled. They also publish a quarterly newsletter. Contact them at P.O. Box 8475, Minneapolis, MN 55408.

Books, Articles, Pamphlets:

Campling, Jo, editor, *Images of Ourselves—Women With Disabilities Talking.* Boston: Routledge and Kegan Paul Ltd., 1981.

Chaussy, Annette, "Deaf Women and the Women's Movement." *The Deaf American*, April 1977.

Connors, Debra, Nanci Stern and Susan Browne, eds. *With the Power of Each Breath*. An anthology of writing by disabled women, forthcoming from Cleis Press in 1985. Write to P.O. Box 8933, Pittsburgh, PA 15221 or P.O. Box 14684, San Francisco, CA 94114.

Egley, Lance. "Domestic Violence and Deaf People: One Community's Approach." *Victimology*. Vol. 7, 1982.

Matthews, Gwyneth Ferguson. *Voices from the Shadows: Women with Disabilities*. Toronto: The Women's Press, 1984.

Melling, Louise. "Wife Abuse in the Deaf Community." *Response to Violence in the Family*, January/February, 1984.

Off Our Backs, Special Issue on Women and Disability, Vol. XI, No. 5, May 1981.

Per-Lee, Myra. *Victim Justice for Disabled Persons: A Resource Manual*. Available for $3.00 plus $1.50 shipping & handling from the Distribution Office, Gallaudet College Press, Kendall Green, Washington, D.C. 20002.

Providing Counseling and Advocacy for Disabled Persons Who Have Been Sexually Abused: A Training Manual for Rape Crisis Center Volunteers. Available from Seattle Rape Relief, 1825 S. Jackson, Suite 102, Seattle WA 98144.

Older Women

Block, Marilyn R. and Jan D. Sinnott, eds. *The Battered Elder Syndrome: An Exploratory Study*. College Park, MD: Center on Aging, University of Maryland, 1979.

Pratt, Clara C., James Koval and Sally Lloyd. "Service workers' responses to abuse of the elderly." *Social Casework*, 1983 (March), Vol. 64 (3), pp. 147–153.

Teen-Aged Women

Brockopp, Karen Susan, Esther Ruth Chew and Nona Kathryn O'Keefe. "A Descriptive Study of Intra-Couple Dating Violence at the High School Level." Unpublished Ph.D. thesis. For more information write to: Esther Chew, P.O. Box 161356, Sacramento, CA 95816.

Davidson, Sue, ed. *The Second Mile: Contemporary Approaches in Counseling Young Women*. Seattle: New Directions for Young Women, 1983. This book is an anthology of articles on needs of young women, including Latina, lesbian, disabled, and abused young women. Available from New Directions for Young Women, 312 S. Washington, Seattle, WA 98104.

NiCarthy, Ginny. *Assertion Skills for Young Women: A Manual*. Seattle: New Directions for Young Women, 1981. Available from NDYW, 312 S. Washington, Seattle, WA 98104.

Religion

Fortune, Marie, *Sexual Violence: The Unmentionable Sin: An Ethical and Pastoral Perspective*. New York: Pilgrim Press, 1983.

Fortune, Marie and Denise Hormann. *Family Violence: Manual for Clergy and Other Service Providers*. Seattle: The Center for the Prevention of Sexual and Domestic Violence (1914 N. 34th, #205, Seattle, WA 98103), 1980.

Alcoholism

Black, Claudia. *It Will Never Happen to Me: Children of Alcoholics*. Denver: MAC Publishing (1850 High Street), 1981.

Swallow, Jean, ed. *Out From Under: Sober Dykes and Our Friends*. San Francisco: Spinsters Ink (803 De Haro, San Francisco, CA 94107), 1983.

Counseling Theory and Leading Groups

Acosta, Frank A., Joe Yamamoto and Leonard Evans. *Effective psychotherapy for low-income and minority patients*. New York: Plenum Press, 1982.

Becerra, Rosina, Marvin Karno, and Javier Escobar, eds. *Mental Health and Hispanic Americans*. New York: Grune and Stratton, 1982.

Beck, Aaron T. *Cognitive Therapy and the Emotional Disorders*. New York: The New American Library, 1976.

Beck, Aaron T., John A. Rush, Brian F. Shaw and Gary Emery. *Cognitive Therapy of Depression*. New York: Guilford Press, 1979.

Berne, Eric, MD. *Principles of Group Treatment*. New York: Grove Press, 1966.

Darty, Trudy and Sandee Potter, eds. *Women Identified Women*. Palo Alto, CA: Mayfield Publishing, 1984.

"Ethnicity in Social Group Work Practice." *Social Work with Groups*. Vol. 7, No. 3, New York: Haworth Press, 1983.

Fish, Dale E. and S. Mae Smith. "Disability: A variable in counselor effectiveness and attitudes toward a disabled person." *Rehabilitation Counseling Bulletin*, 1983 (Volume 2, Number 2), pp. 120–123.

Froland, Charles and Diane L. Pancoast, eds. *Networks for Helping: Illustrations from Research and Practice*. Portland, OR: Natural Helping Networks Project, Regional Research Institute, Portland State University, 1978.

Johnson, David W. and Frank P. Johnson. *Joining Together: Group Therapy and Group Skills*. Englewood Cliffs, NJ: Prentice-Hall, Inc., 1975.

Katz, Alfred H. and Eugene I. Bender. *The Strength in Us: Self-Help Groups in the Modern World*. New York: New Viewpoints (Div. of Franklin Watts), 1976.

Keller, Peter A. and Dennis J. Murray. *Handbook of Rural Community Mental Health*. New York: Human Sciences Press, 1982.

Lange, Arthur J. and Patricia Jakubowski. *Responsible Assertive Behavior: Cognitive/Behavioral Procedures for Trainers*. Champaign, IL: Research Press, 1977.

Moses, A. Elfin and Robert O. Hawkins, Jr. *Counseling Lesbian Women and Gay Men*. St. Louis: C. V. Mosby Co., 1982.

Reed, Beth Glover and Charles D. Garvin, guest editors. *Groupwork with Women/Groupwork with Men: An Overview of Gender Issues in Social Groupwork Practice*. Social Work with Groups, Vol. 6, Nos. 3/4. New York: Haworth Press, 1983.

Shaw, Linda. *Counseling the Abuse Victim*. Harrisburg, PA: The Pennsylvania Coalition Against Domestic Violence, undated.

Slavson, S. R. *The Fields of Group Psychotherapy*. New York: Schocken Books, 1971.

Sue, Stanley and James Morishima. *The Mental Health of Asian Americans*. San Francisco: Jossey Bass Publishers, 1982.

Feminist Theory and Feminist Therapy

de Beauvoir, Simone. *The Second Sex*. New York: Alfred A. Knopf, 1952.

Chesler, Phyllis. *Women and Madness*. New York: Avon Books, 1973.

Delacoste, Frederique and Felice Newman, eds. *Fight Back: Feminist Resistance to Male Violence*. Minneapolis: Cleis Press, 1981. Available from Cleis Press, P.O. Box 8933, Pittsburgh, PA 15221 or P.O. Box 14684, San Francisco, CA 94114.

Dinnerstein, Dorothy. *The Mermaid and the Minotaur: Sexual Arrangements and the Human Malaise*. New York: Harper and Row, 1976.

Eichenbaum, Luise and Orbach, Susie. *What Do Women Want*. New York: Coward-McCann, 1983.

Friedan, Betty. *The Feminine Mystique*. New York: W. W. Norton & Co., Inc., 1963.

Gilligan, Carol. *In a Different Voice*. Cambridge, MA: Harvard University Press, 1982.

Gornick, Vivian and Moran, Barbara. *Woman in Sexist Society*. New York: Basic Books, 1971.

Gottlieb, Naomi, ed. *Alternative Social Services for Women*. New York: Columbia University Press, 1980.

Hyde, Janet Shibley and B. G. Rosenberg. *Half the Human Experience: The Psychology of Women*. Lexington, MA: D.C. Heath, 1976.

Joseph, Gloria I. and Jill Lewis. *Common Differences: Conflicts in Black and White Feminist Perspectives*. Garden City, New York: Anchor Books/Doubleday, 1981.

Kaplan, Alexandra. "Androgyny as a Model of Mental Health for Women: From Theory to Therapy," in Kaplan, A. and J. Bean, *Beyond Sex-Role Stereotypes*. Boston: Little, Brown & Co., 1976.

Mander, Anica Vesel and Anne Kent Rush. *Feminism as Therapy*. New York: Random House, Inc., 1974.

Miller, Jean Baker. *Toward a New Psychology of Women*. Boston: Beacon Press, 1976.

Morgan, Robin, ed. *Sisterhood is Powerful: An Anthology of Writings from the Women's Liberation Movement*. New York: Random House, 1970.

Pogrebin, Letty Cottin. *Family Politics*. New York: McGraw-Hill, 1982.

Pogrebin, Letty Cottin. *Growing Up Free*. New York: Bantam Books, 1981.

Rawlings, Edna I. and Carter, Dianne K. *Psychotherapy for Women, Treatment toward Equality*. Springfield, IL: Charles C. Thomas, 1977.

Robbins, Joan Hammerman and Rachel Josefowitz Siegel, guest editors. *Women Changing Therapy: New Assessments, Values and Strategies in Feminist Therapy*. (*Women & Therapy*, Volume 2, Number 2/3). New York: Haworth Press, 1983.

Rubin, Lillian. *Intimate Strangers*. New York: Harper & Row, 1983.

Safilios-Rothschild, Constantina. *Love, Sex and Sex Roles*. Englewood Cliffs, NJ: Prentice-Hall, 1977.

Thomas, Susan Amelia. "Theory and Practice in Feminist Therapy," *Social Work*, November, 1977.

Williams, Elizabeth. *Notes of a Feminist Therapist*. New York: Dell, 1976.

Self-Help

Armstrong, Louise. *Kiss Daddy Goodnight: A Speak Out on Incest*. New York: Pocket Books, 1978.

Azibo, Aloni and Therese Crylen Unumb. *The Mature Woman's Back-to-Work Book*. Chicago: Contemporary Books, Inc., 1980.

Barbach, Lonnie and Linda Levine. *Shared Intimacies*. New York: Bantam Books, 1982.

Berzon, Betty and Robert Leighton. *Positively Gay*. Milbrae, CA: Celestial Arts, 1979.

Black, Claudia. *It Will Never Happen to Me: Children of Alcoholics*. Denver, CO: M.A.C. Publications (1850 High Street), 1981.

Boston Women's Health Book Collective. *Our Bodies, Ourselves*. New York: Simon and Schuster, 1979.

Briggs, Dorothy Corkille. *Your Child's Self-Esteem*. New York: Doubleday. 1975.

Burns, David. *Feeling Good*. New York: Signet, 1980.

Butler, Pamela E. *Talking to Yourself: Learning the Language of Self-Support*. San Francisco: Harper & Row, 1981.

Catalyst, the Staff of. *What to Do with the Rest of Your Life*. New York: Simon and Schuster, 1981.

Edwards, Marie and Eleanor Hoover. *The Challenge of Being Single*. New York: New American Library, Inc., 1974.

Francke, Linda Bird. *Growing Up Divorced*. New York: Simon and Schuster, 1983.

Gardner, Richard, MD. *The Boys and Girls Book about Divorce*. New York: Bantam Books, 1980.

Gendlin, Eugene. *Focusing*. New York: Bantam Books, 1981.

Goldstine, Daniel et al. *The Dance-Away Lover*. William Morrow & Co., 1977.

Halpern, Howard. *How to Break Your Addiction to a Person*. New York: Bantam Books, 1982.

Krantzler, Mel. *Learning to Love Again*. New York: Bantam Books, 1979.

Kushner, Harold S. *When Bad Things Happen to Good People*. New York: Avon, 1983.

Lazarre, Jane. *The Mother Knot*. New York: Dell, 1976.

McGinnis, Alan Loy. *The Friendship Factor: How to Get Closer to the People You Care For*. Minneapolis: Augsburg Publishing House, 1979.

Newman, Mildred and Bernard Berkowitz. *How to Be Your Own Best Friend*. New York: Ballantine Books, 1971.

NiCarthy, Ginny. *Getting Free: A Handbook for Women in Abusive Relationships*. Seattle: Seal Press, 1982.

Peck, M. Scott. *The Road Less Traveled: A New Psychology of Love, Traditional Values and Spiritual Growth*. New York: Touchstone (Simon and Schuster), 1978.

Peele, Stanton. *How Much Is Too Much*. Englewood Cliffs, NJ: Prentice-Hall, 1981.

Peele, Stanton. *Love and Addiction*. New York: Signet Books, 1975.

Phillips, Dr. Debora. *How to Fall Out of Love*. New York: Fawcett, 1978.

Sonkin, Daniel Jay and Michael Durphy. *Learning to Live Without Violence: A Handbook for Men*. San Francisco: Volcano Press, 1982.

Tavris, Carol. *Anger: The Misunderstood Emotion*. New York: Simon & Schuster, 1982.

Ternsterhein, Herbert and Jean Baer. *Don't Say Yes When You Want to Say No*. New York: Dell Pub., 1975.

Wanderer, Zev and Tracy Cabot. *Letting Go*. New York: Warner Books, 1978.

Wetherby, Terry. *Conversations: Working Women Talk about Doing a "Man's Job."* Millbrae, CA: Les Femmes Publishing, 1977.

Zimbardo, Phillip G. *Shyness*. New York: Jove Pub., Inc., 1977.

Organizations

National Clearinghouse on Marital Rape, 2325 Oak Street, Berkeley, CA 94708.

National Clearinghouse on Domestic Violence, P.O. Box 2309, Rockville, MD 20852. Collects and disseminates free information on the incidence and causes of domestic violence, as well as available programs and services.

National Coalition Against Sexual Assault. For information contact NCASA, c/o Austin Rape Crisis Center, P.O. Box 7156, Austin, TX 78713. A national network of rape crisis centers.

National Coalition Against Domestic Violence, 2401 Virginia Avenue, N.W., Suite 306, Washington, D.C. 20037. A national network of battered women's programs. NCADV also has many member state coalitions throughout the country. Contact the national office for information on resources in your area.

Resource Center on Family Violence, Center for Women Policy Studies, 2000 P Street NW, Suite 508, Washington, DC 20036. Provides materials, publications and technical assistance to people working in the domestic violence field. Also publishes a newsletter, *Response to Violence in the Family*.

About the Authors:

Ginny NiCarthy, MSW, has led groups for abused women since 1976 and has conducted workshops on a variety of women's issues in the United States, England and Scotland. The author of *Getting Free: A Handbook for Women in Abusive Relationships* and *The Ones Who Got Away: Women Who Left Abusive Partners,* NiCarthy is currently a counselor with The Women's Counseling Group in Seattle.

Karen Merriam, MSW, ACSW, has worked in the field of sexual and domestic violence since 1977. Merriam is currently leading groups for battered women and for women who experienced sexual abuse in childhood, and is director of Trauma Health Services in Seattle.

Sandra Coffman, Ph.D., is a psychologist with The Women's Counseling Group in Seattle. She has led groups for battered women and has worked at the University of Washington and for a variety of community agencies serving women.

Chain Chain Change

For Black Women Dealing With
Physical and Emotional Abuse

by EVELYN C. WHITE

No shelter or agency, no counselor or activist dealing with Black women in abusive relationships should be without this ground-breaking book. Meant to be used both by the battered woman herself and by those who work with her, CHAIN CHAIN CHANGE offers practical advice for recognizing the signs of abuse, dealing with the police and the legal system, getting support from family, friends and the church.

The author, Black journalist Evelyn C. White, a former victim advocate for the Seattle City Attorney's Battered Women's Project, analyzes Black women's self-image, the batterer's syndrome as it applies to Black men in our society, racism in shelters and other challenging topics.

Incorporating quotes by writers Ntozake Shange and Toni Morrison and singer Aretha Franklin, as well as brief interviews with formerly battered Black women, this book carries a strong message of self-affirming change.

"This book is to help Black women understand that our silence will not protect us and that no amount of real or imagined strength can shield us from mortal harm."

"Shelters must make changes. For they are perceived now, by many Black women, as just another place where white people try to run our lives and tell us what to do."

76 pages, paperback
$4.95
ISBN: 0-931188-25-3

Mejor Sola Que Mal Acompañada

Para la Mujer Golpeada/
For the Latina in an Abusive Relationship

by MYRNA M. ZAMBRANO

MEJOR SOLA QUE MAL ACOMPAÑADA is the first bilingual Spanish-English book to approach the problem of abuse from a Latina perspective. With an emphasis on alternatives for the battered woman, *Mejor Sola* is an extremely useful guide for her and an invaluable support to counselors, shelter workers and activists working with a Hispanic population. Straightforward and informative, *Mejor Sola* covers the dilemmas posed for the undocumented woman, the woman with few resources, and the woman who speaks little or no English. The adjoining Spanish and English texts complement each other, and are especially helpful in familiarizing Spanish-speaking women with necessary English terms and teaching Anglos the equivalent phrases in Spanish.

Myrna M. Zambrano, a graduate of Yale University, is the daughter of naturalized Mexican parents. She has been part of the movement against rape and domestic violence for many years, working to help Latinas as a bilingual counselor, educator and public speaker.

241 pages, paperback
$7.95
ISBN: 0-931188-26-1

Getting Free:

A Handbook for Women in Abusive Relationships

by GINNY NICARTHY

Now in its expanded, second edition, GETTING FREE is the first book directed to the abused woman herself. Written by an experienced counselor and workshop leader, it's a self-help handbook that provides practical advice for overcoming fears, for finding shelter, for dealing with the batterer and with the children, for evaluating lawyers, doctors and counselors, and for finding new friends and relationships. GETTING FREE includes forty exercises and questionnaires and a helpful reading list. Thousands of shelter workers and counselors have found GETTING FREE invaluable, and it is essential reading for any woman in an abusive relationship.

"Directed to the battered woman herself, *Getting Free* will doubtless also prove useful to those who deal with her, either personally or professionaly. . . . Highly recommended."
— *Library Journal*

"Those of us who counsel women on the crisis line and in the shelter are painfully aware of the struggle the woman goes through to leave an abusive relationship. Ginny Nicarthy has come up with a flexible, practical handbook for all of us to use. . . . Get a hold of it and read it!"
— *A Safe Place Newsletter*

316 pages, paperback
$10.95
ISBN: 0-931188-37-7